FOX 13

ONE TANK TRIPS®

Fun Florida Adventures

Seaside
Publishing, Inc.

One Tank Trips® is a publication conceived and developed by WTVT FOX13 and published by Seaside Publishing Inc., a division of Famous Florida Enterprises, Inc.

PUBLISHER
Joyce LaFray - Seaside Publishing

PRODUCTION & DESIGN
Kevin Coccaro - FOX13
Jim Wahl - FOX13
Kim Seymour - FOX13
Mo Eppley - Seaside Publishing

CONTRIBUTING WRITERS & EDITORS
Vicki Krueger - Seaside Publishing
FOX13 Staff

SEASIDE PUBLISHING STAFF
Patricia Mack - Senior Editor
Steven Groth - VP, Sales & Marketing

Additional copies of this book may be ordered by calling
1-888-ONE-TANK (663-8265)
Visit our Web site to order online at:
www.FoxOneTankTrips.com or **www.SeasidePublishing.com**
Or you may write Seaside Publishing at:
P.O. Box 14441, St. Petersburg, FL 33733

ISBN: 978-0-9760555-2-5
Library of Congress Catalog Number: 2008909892
© 2009 New World Communications of Tampa, Inc.

Photography - Front cover: '55 Chevy BelAir (© Jim Wahl), 1955 Chevy courtesy of P.J.'s Classic Autos. Back cover clockwise left to right: Tarpon Springs sponge diver (© St. Petersburg/Clearwater CVB); Fort De Soto Beach (© St. Petersburg/Clearwater CVB); Lowry Park Zoo Elephants (© Lowry Park Zoo); Mount Dora Sunset (© Mount Dora Chamber of Commerce).
Interior photography - All photos copyright WTVT FOX13 unless indicated otherwise.
Title page photos - Top to bottom: Fort De Soto Beach (© St. Petersburg/Clearwater CVB); Tarpon Springs sponge diver (© St. Petersburg/Clearwater CVB); Tampa's Lowry Park Zoo Elephants (© Lowry Park Zoo).

Special thanks to: Georgia Turner & Associates, Geiger & Associates, St. Petersburg/Clearwater CVB, Stuart Newman & Associates, Cindy Cockburn.

Special Sales: Bulk purchases (12+ copies) for FOX13 TAMPA BAY'S ONE TANK TRIPS® are available to companies at special discounts. For more information call Steven Groth, Vice President, Sales & Marketing at 1-888-ONE-TANK (663-8265) or write to Seaside Publishing, Special Sales P.O. Box 14441, St. Petersburg, FL 33733.

Acknowledgments

One Tank Trips® reflects the contributions of the dedicated staff at **FOX13**. This travel guide would not have been possible without the special efforts of:

Bill Schneider
Vice President & General Manager

Mike McClain
Vice President of News

Phil Metlin
Former Vice President of News

Mike House
Vice President of Creative Services

Jim Wahl
Design Director

Kim Seymour
Senior Designer

Kevin Coccaro
Broadcast & Multimedia Designer

Carrie Schroeder
Promotion/Community Affairs Manager

A special thanks to:

Carolyn Forrest
Vice President, FTS

And every member of the FOX13 team

CONTENTS

CONTENTS

FLORIDA MAP

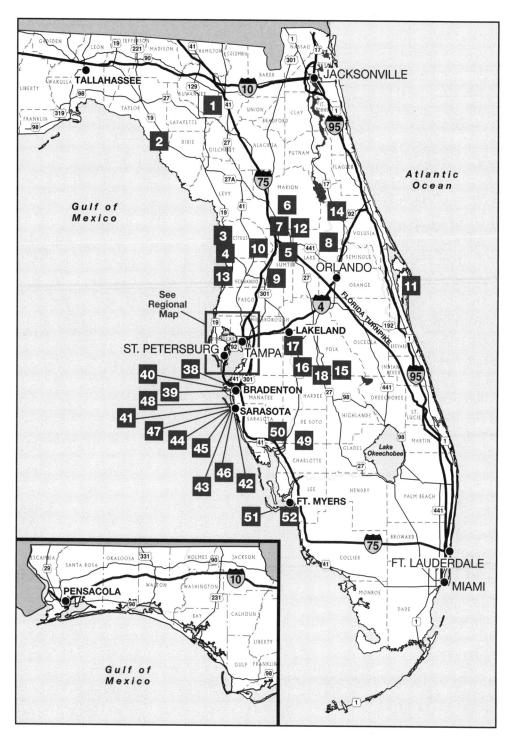

REGIONAL MAP

One Tank Trips

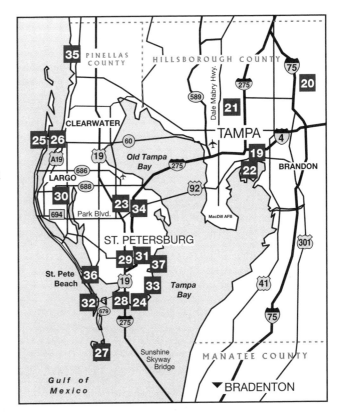

Discover the *real* Florida

At **WTVT FOX13,** we enjoy taking viewers to off-the-beaten path travel spots. There is a good reason tourism is Florida's top industry. This picturesque state is populated with vibrant and interesting people. **One Tank Trips®** is designed to help you discover the best places and plan your own outings in the Tampa Bay area.

Whether you are headed to the quaint town of Micanopy to hunt for antiques, to Fort DeSoto Park for an historic stroll or to the Greek town of Tarpon Springs to watch the famous Epiphany cross tossing ceremony, you will always want to have this handy guide at your side.

This unique travel book will satisfy anyone and everyone with an unrelenting wanderlust for discovering the *real* Florida. It is packed with information you need for an enjoyable outing, including travel tips and detailed maps. For quick access keep it in your glove compartment. You will find it is a necessity!

"One Tank Trips®" is a proud part of the **WTVT FOX13** family and we know it will become a part of yours. So buckle up and enjoy 52 of Florida's best destinations, reachable on just one tank of gas.

For more than half a century, **WTVT FOX13** has been broadcasting unique stories about interesting and scenic destinations across Florida. Our state is famous for its beaches, theme parks and other tourist attractions. Many of the best places are easy to visit on a single tank of gas, so we decided to come up with a feature segment called **"One Tank Trip®."** Response from viewers was tremendous and switchboard operators were overwhelmed by calls from people seeking information, directions, phone numbers and admission prices. We knew we had a hit on our hands and decided to create a guide book that highlighted 52 of the best destinations within one tank of gas of the Bay Area.

We hope you like discovering these adventures and attractions across the state as much as we have.

Enjoy this handy travel guide and be sure to watch **FOX13's "Good Day Tampa Bay"** for your next **One Tank Trip®!**

Bill Schneider
Vice President & General Manager
WTVT FOX13 Television

Florida Fairs

Florida's fantastic weather permits year-round celebrations at a variety of festivals and fairs. Here's a brief month-by-month calendar of just a few of the most popular events, many focused on historic traditions and foods indigenous to Florida. Be sure to check ahead to confirm that the event has not been rescheduled. Visit the Web sites listed or call for specific information, dates and times.

JANUARY

Annual Kiwanis Medieval Faire, Ft. Myers.
www.medieval-faire.com
(239)839-8036

Kumquat Festival, Dade City.
www.kumquatfestival.org
(352)567-3769

FEBRUARY

Florida State Fair, Tampa.
www.floridastatefair.com
(800)345-3247

Florida Strawberry Festival, Plant City.
www.flstrawberryfestival.com
(813)752-9194

Gasparilla Piratefest Invasion & Parade, Tampa.
www.gasparillapiratefest.com
(813)237-3258

South Beach Wine & Food Festival, Miami.
www.sobewineandfoodfest.com
(305)229-5249

MARCH

Annual Easter Boogie & World Record Dives, Zephyrhills.
www.mainstreetzephyrhills.org
(813)780-1414

Festival of States, St. Petersburg.
www.festivalofstates.com
(727)321-9888

Grant Seafood Festival, Grant.
www.grantseafoodfestival.com
(321)723-8687

Winter Park Sidewalk Art Festival, Winter Park.
www.wpsaf.org
(407)790-0597

APRIL

Cedar Key Arts Festival, Cedar Key.
www.cedarkeyartsfestival.com
(352)543-5400

Tampa Bay Blues Fest, St.Petersburg.
www.tampabaybluesfest.com
(727)502-5000

MAY

Blue Crab Festival, Downtown Palatka.
www.bluecrabfestival.com
(386)325-4406

Florida Folk Festival, White Springs.
www.floridafolkfestival.com
(877)635-3655

Ruskin Tomato & Heritage Festival, Ruskin.
www.ruskintomatofestival.org
(813)645-3808

Zellwood Sweet Corn Festival, Zellwood.
www.zellwoodcornfestival.com
(407)886-0014

and Festivals

JUNE

Cuban American Heritage Festival,
Key West.
www.cubanfest.com
(305)295-9665

Chiefland Watermelon Festival,
Chiefland.
www.chieflandwatermelonfestival.com
(352)493-0911

JULY

International Mango Festival,
Homestead.
www.fairchildgarden.org
(305)258-0464

AUGUST

Greek Winefest, Tarpon Springs.
www.spongedocks.net/tarpon-springs-
events.htm
(813)629-8304

SEPTEMBER

Mid Florida Balloon Festival, Eustis.
www.midfloridaballoonfestival.com
(407)886-5393

Pensacola Seafood Festival,
Pensacola.
www.visitpensacola.com
(850)432-1450

OCTOBER

**Biketoberfest for motorcycling
enthusiasts,** Daytona Beach.
www.biketoberfest.org
(866)296-8970

John's Pass Seafood Festival,
Madeira Beach.
www.johnspass.com
(727)397-9764

**Cedar Key at the Birding &
Wildlife Experience.**
www.ncbwe.com
(352)543-5600

Fall Harvest & Peanut Festival,
Williston.
www.willistonfl.com
(352)528-5552

San Antonio Rattlesnake Festival.
www.rattlesnakefestival.com
(352)588-4444

**Stone Crab, Seafood & Wine
Festival,** Longboat Key.
www.colonybeachresort.com
1-800-4-COLONY

Swamp Buggy Races, Naples.
www.swampbuggy.com
(239)774-2701

NOVEMBER

Florida Seafood Festival,
Apalachicola.
www.floridaseafoodfestival.com
(850)653-4720

Land O' Lakes Flapjack Festival.
www.centralpascochamber.com
(813)909-2722

Miami Book Fair International,
Miami.
www.miamibookfair.com
(305)237-3258

Plant City Pig Jam, Plant City.
www.plantcitypigjam.com
(813)764-3707

Ribfest, St. Petersburg.
www.ribfest.org
(727)528-3828

DECEMBER

Miccosukee Indians Art Festival,
Miami.
www.miccosukeeresort.com
(305)553-8365

**Pioneer Florida Museum & Village
Christmas Open House,** Dade City.
www.pioneerfloridamuseum.org
(352)562-0262

Ginnie Springs Outdoors

outdoor adventure awaits

Glenda Jones

The clear water of Ginnie Springs will bring out the adventurer in you.

William Dooley

The trip

If Ginnie Springs doesn't have it all, it sure comes close. And the setting is simply gorgeous! A leisurely float down the Santa Fe River will calm the savage beast in you.

What to see

The crystal-clear water in the springs is perfect for a host of water sports. Go canoeing, tubing, snorkeling or scuba diving. You can even launch your boat. Landlubbers will enjoy the wilderness trails. And, if you want to stay awhile, there are 100 camping sites scattered through-out the 200 wooded acres, many have riverfront and spring locations. Some have electric and water hook-ups, heated bathrooms, picnic tables and grills.

Other highlights

Visiting groups of 30 or more can reserve one of the five pavilions locat-ed near the springs. They make a perfect place to meet and picnic. Nearby there are beach-style volleyball courts that are lit in the evenings. Families will enjoy the rustic children's playground near the Ginnie Springs picnic pavilion.

The facts

Ginnie Springs Outdoors
7300 N.E. Ginnie Springs Road
High Springs, FL 32643
(386) 454-7188

Admission: $12 for adults, $3 for children 7 to 14, free for children 6 and younger. Call or visit the Web site for daily admission for scuba diving, camping and cottage rentals.

Hours: Monday through Thursday in summer from 8 a.m. to 7 p.m.; in winter 8 a.m. to 6 p.m. Open Sunday in summer from 8 a.m. to 8 p.m.; in winter 8 a.m. to 7 p.m. Open year-round on Friday and Saturday from 8 a.m. to 10 p.m.

www.ginniespringsoutdoors.com

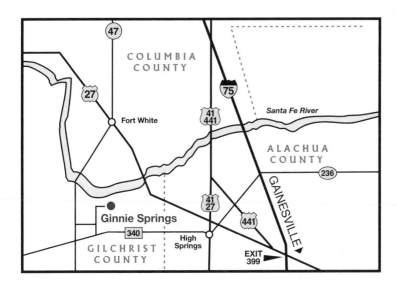

Directions

From Tampa, take Interstate 75 exit 399 (the Alachua exit) to U.S. 441 north approximately 5 miles to the town of High Springs. Turn left onto State Roads 41 & 27. Go south to County Road 340. Look for signs indicating the turnoff for Ginnie, Blue and Poe Springs. Turn right onto C.R. 340 and go west approximately 6.5 miles to the Ginnie Springs turnoff on the right. Travel approximately 1 mile to the Ginnie Springs Outdoors entrance.

Jacques Cousteau said of his visit to the waters of Ginnie Springs: "Visibility forever!" He was right.

Steinhatchee Scallop Dive

nature's bounty

The tranquil waters of the Steinhatchee River yield a bumper crop of lush, savory scallops. No matter how you cook your catch, Florida scallops are a taste treat.

The trip

Along the winding backroads of northern Florida, you'll find this small fishing village. The catch of the summer is always bay scallops.

What to see

Before you get in the water, you'll need to obtain a saltwater fishing license which can be purchased at any nearby marina. If you don't get one before you go, you can get one at any of the marinas in Steinhatchee. To find the scallops, you'll need a pair of fins, a mask and a snorkel. As a first-time scalloper, you'll find it has nothing to do with fishing. It's all about gathering. However, there is a legal limit on how much you gather. Please check the latest information before you head out.

Boats can be chartered at a nearby marina. A bumper crop of scallops nestles in the shallow waters where the Steinhatchee River meets the Gulf of Mexico. The vast underworld of sea grass is fertile ground for scallops. Some are easy to find. Others are more elusive. But don't worry, they don't bite.

Other highlights

Time to shuck your catch. Maybe you'll discover you have a natural talent for prying open the shells. Once you're done, you can cook your catch. Broiled or fried, there's nothing better than fresh-cooked Florida scallops.

The facts

Steinhatchee Landing Resort
203 Ryland Circle
Steinhatchee, FL 32359
(352) 498-3513

Admission: *The resort rents 1 to 4 bedroom cottages for 2-night or longer stays.*

Hours: *Scallop season varies. It's usually from the beginning of July to September 10. Call the resort to check.*

www.steinhatcheelanding.com

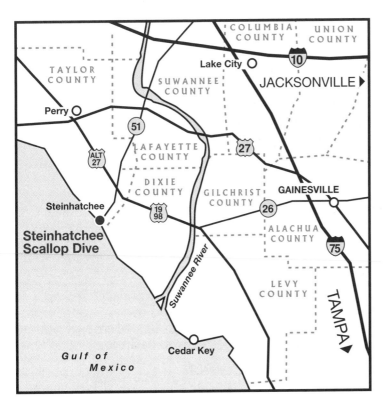

Directions

From Tampa, take Interstate 75 north to the Brooksville exit and follow U.S. 98 north to U.S. 19. Follow U.S. 19 north to Taylor County. Take State Road 51 in Taylor County west to Steinhatchee.

This is a taste of Florida in a tiny fishing village.

Crystal River
Swim with the Manatees

up close with the gentle giants

The Crystal River area is famous around the world as a haven for manatees.

The trip

Swimming with the manatees is something you'll remember for a long time. It is a not-to-be missed experience on your visit to Crystal River in Citrus County.

What to see

The best time of year to see manatees begins in November and ends in March. That's when water in the Gulf of Mexico is coolest, so the manatees head to the warm spring water near Kings Bay. Make sure you go early in the morning. Manatees are more likely to be around at that time.

The guides are Diana and Bill Oestreich, the co-owners of Birds Underwater, a dive shop that offers manatee tours. They will tell you how to make friends with the sea giants.

Other highlights

Explore the Bird's Underwater Gift Shop that sells calendars, stuffed animals, cool magnets and memorable manatee videos. Or, tour Kings Bay on an enclosed pontoon boat. It's a three-hour wonder!

The facts

Crystal River
Swim with the Manatees
Birds Underwater Dive Shop
320 N.W. U.S. 19
Crystal River, FL 34428
(352) 563-2763
Toll free: (800) 771-2763

Admission: *Call for tour and equipment rental rates.*

Hours: *Main tour meets at 6:15 a.m. Call for dive times, tour availability and reservations that are required.*

www.birdsunderwater.com

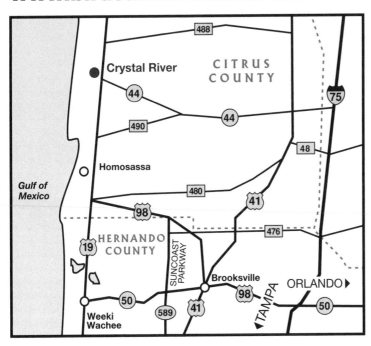

Directions

From Tampa, take Interstate 75 north and exit on U.S. 98 west, which will take you to U.S. 19. Head north on U.S. 19 toward Crystal River. Birds Underwater is half a mile north of County Road 44 on the south side of the road, behind Dockside Trading Co.

Swim with the herd, the manatee herd!

Homosassa Springs Wildlife State Park

fall in love with the manatees

From The Fish Bowl, the park's underwater observatory, you can see manatees and other marine life.

The trip

Just off U.S.19, away from the cars and strip malls, sits a natural treasure. Let a pontoon boat take you up Pepper Creek and back to the "real" Florida. At the headwater of the river sits this 210-acre park, preserving and protecting Florida wildlife.

What to see

What a perfect place to see manatees! The Manatee Education Center is a halfway house for injured and orphaned manatees. They'll recover here until they're well enough to be released. Through the park's underwater observatory, you get to see these gentle giants and a rich variety of other marine life.

Other highlights

Enjoy the sights and sounds of nature in the park that animals have made their home. Trails offer views of deer, bear, bobcats and a variety of tropical birds in their native habitat. There's also a great little gift shop.

The facts

Homosassa Springs Wildlife State Park
4150 S. Suncoast Blvd.
Homosassa, FL 34446
(352) 628-2311

Admission: *$9 adults, $5 children 3 to 12, free for children younger than 3.*

Hours: *Although the park is open daily 9 a.m. to 5:30 p.m., plan to arrive before 1 p.m. to enjoy all of its facilities. Ticket sales end at 4 p.m.*

www.homosassasprings.org

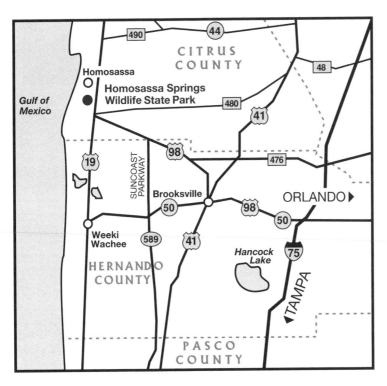

Directions

From Tampa, take Interstate 75 north and exit on U.S. 98 west that will take you to U.S. 19. Head north on U.S. 19. The visitor center and main entrance to Homosassa Springs Wildlife State Park is on U.S. 19 in Homosassa Springs.

Escape the real Florida of today for the real Florida of days gone by.

Lakeridge Winery & Vineyards

a taste of the sweet life

Lakeridge Winery & Vineyards

Lakeridge Winery makes its wines from grapes developed to grow in Florida's climate.

The trip

What a wonderful surprise! Florida's largest winery and vineyards overlooks the rolling hills of south Lake County. And the Spanish-style Lakeridge Winery building is beautiful.

What to see

Your visit will begin with a tour of the winery and a look at the vineyards. You'll learn that (with all due respect to California and New York) the first recorded reference to wine made from New World grapes was to those grown near Jacksonville.

After the tour, it's time to do some tasting. Lakeridge has won many awards for its wines. Right now it produces several very good whites and two red, most on the sweet side.

Other highlights

In the gift shop you can buy wine and wine-related items — wine glasses, corkscrews and even clothing celebrating wine! There's also a picnic area. So bring along some cheese and the romantic in you, and enjoy the sweeter side of life.

The facts

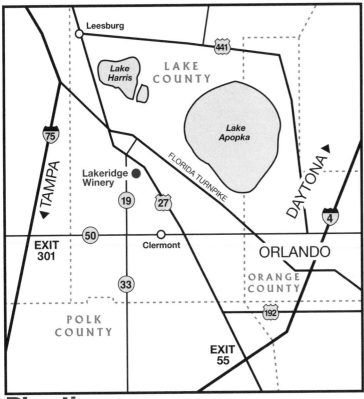

Lakeridge Winery & Vineyard
19239 U.S. 27 N.
Clermont, FL 34715
(352) 394-8627
Toll free: (800) 768-WINE (9463)

Admission: *Free.*

Hours: *Monday through Saturday 10 a.m. to 5 p.m.,*
Sunday 11 a.m. to 5 p.m.
Closed on major holidays.

www.lakeridgewinery.com

Directions

From Tampa, take Interstate 75 north to exit 301 (Route 50) east and turn north on U.S. 27 to the winery. From Interstate 4 take exit 55 to Route 50. Turn north on U.S. 27 to the winery.

This place is very 'tasteful.'

Marjorie Kinnan Rawlings Historic State Park

6

a place of inspiration

Marjorie Kinnan Rawlings State Historic Site

Marjorie Kinnan Rawlings drew the inspiration for her books from her home at Cross Creek. Original kitchen at the Marjorie Kinnan Rawlings homestead.

J. LaFray

The trip

"I don't know how anyone can live without some place of enchantment to turn to." For author Marjorie Kinnan Rawlings, that place was her home at Cross Creek.

What to see

This Cracker-style house and farm is where Marjorie Kinnan Rawlings wrote "The Yearling," a novel that won the Pulitzer Prize in 1939. Today you can still feel her presence as you tour the house and grounds. Step out on the veranda and take a deep breath. The air is full of the scents of pine and citrus that instilled her love for Florida. It's on this veranda, where her typewriter still sits, that she did most of her writing — inspired by the magic of this place.

Other highlights

Not far from Cross Creek is the charming community of Micanopy — an antique lover's paradise.

The facts

Marjorie Kinnan Rawlings Historic State Park
18700 South County Road #325
Cross Creek, FL 32640
(352) 466-3672

Admission: $2 per carload, 8 people maximum. Admission for house tours is $3 adults, $2 children 6 to 12, free for 5 and younger.

Hours: The house is open to the public only through tours on Thursday through Sunday on the hour at 10 a.m., 11 a.m., 1, 2, 3 and 4 p.m. Tours are offered October through July; no tours are conducted in August and September. The yard, citrus grove and nature trails are open year-round from 9 a.m. to 5 p.m. daily. Closed Thanksgiving and Christmas.

www.floridastateparks.org/ marjoriekinnanrawlings

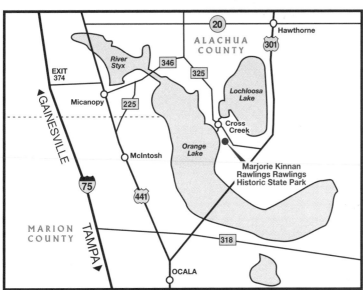

Directions

From Tampa, take Interstate 75 north to exit 374 (Micanopy), heading east towards U.S. 441. Turn right on U.S. 441 and go about 1 mile to County Road 346. Turn left and go 4 or 5 miles to C. R. 325. Turn right. The historic site is about 4 miles on the right.

The enchanting Cracker home and inspiration for a truly remarkable woman.

Micanopy

beauty comes in small packages

The lovely Herlong Mansion is a cozy bed and breakfast with 12 bedrooms and private baths. The nearby museum at Micanopy proudly displays the five flags that have flown over Florida.

The trip

Just 30 minutes north of Ocala, you'll come upon the historic town of Micanopy, Florida's oldest inland settlement. The town's setting is one of beauty and charm. Named for Chief Micanopy, this little town is now one of the premier antique centers in the state.

What to see

In the mood for furniture, a cameo or a good book? You're sure to find just the thing in one of Micanopy's many antique and curio stores. Just strolling down the street makes you feel as though you've gone back to a simpler time. The museum features a talking map detailing aspects of Spanish and African-American history in Florida.

Other highlights

All that shopping will make you hungry. Fortunately, there's great food in and around Micanopy, whether you're in the mood for a quick sandwich, pizza, barbecue, a scoop of ice cream or a full-fledged meal. And if you want to stay awhile, try the Herlong for a memorable stay.

The facts

Micanopy Historical Society Museum
Cholokka Boulevard & Bay Street
Micanopy, FL 32667
(352) 466-3200

Admission: *$2 donation suggested.*

Hours: *Daily 1 p.m. to 4 p.m. Closed Christmas Day and Thanksgiving. Stores are open daily, although some are closed on Tuesdays. Most close on major holidays. Restaurant hours vary.*

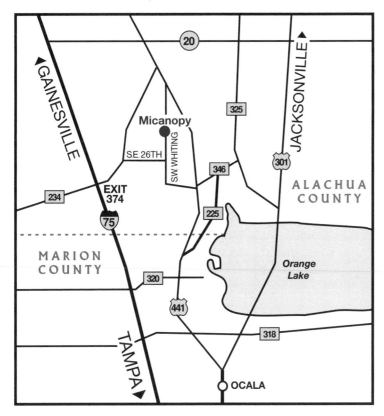

Directions

From Tampa, take Interstate 75 north to exit 374 toward Micanopy. Turn right onto County Road 234. Turn right onto S.E. 26th St. Turn left onto S.W. Whiting St. and go 1 mile east to downtown.

Here's a little piece of the world you can enjoy for a few hours or for a weekend getaway.

Mount Dora

treat yourself to this place

Mount Dora Area Chamber of Commerce

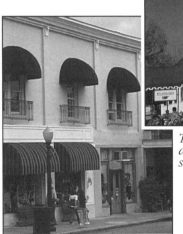

This charming lakefront town is perfect for antiquing, shopping and sightseeing. The shops are quaint and the house historic.

The trip

Mount Dora has been called many things: the New England of the South, the Antique Center of Central Florida and the City of Parks, among others. You can boat from Lake Dora all the way to the Atlantic, but as beautiful as this place is, why leave?

What to see

Nearly 75 gift shops, antique shops, art shops and boutiques call Mount Dora home. On weekends, stop by Renninger's Antique Market. It has more than 700 hand-picked vendors. Visit the indoor Flea Market next door to Renninger's, for some superb bargains.

Other highlights

You can't beat the parks in Mount Dora. The nature path at Palm Island Park leads you along the lake so you can enjoy nature's rich offerings. If you prefer beauty created by human hands, Mount Dora features some breathtaking buildings. Check out the Donnelly House. It displays Queen Anne architecture with a wrap-around porch and gingerbread trim. A night at the historic Lakeside Inn will be a memorable experience. And the Windsor Rose English Tea House offers a great cup of fresh-brewed tea.

The facts

Mount Dora
Mount Dora Area
Chamber of Commerce
341 N. Alexander St.
Mount Dora, FL 32757
(352) 383-2165

Hours: *Shop and restaurant hours vary.*

www.mountdora.com

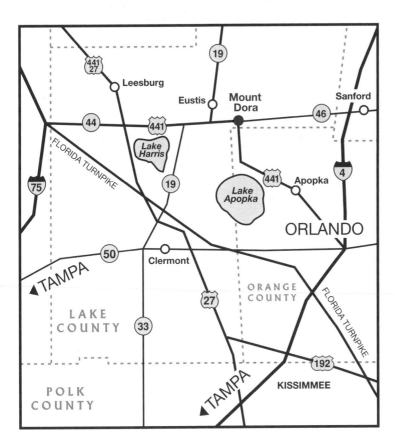

Directions

From Tampa, take Interstate 75 north to County Road 44 east to U.S. 441 south to Mount Dora. From Interstate 4, take U.S. 441 north to Mount Dora.

Mount Dora is as compelling a setting as anywhere in the state.

Pioneer Florida Museum & Village

a taste of old Florida

The Lacoochee School has been restored and furnished to depict a one-room school house.

The trip

If you're not a fan of museums, don't let the word scare you. You'll spend happy hours here in buildings that let you experience life in Florida during the 1800s and early 1900s.

What to see

This place is a history buff's dream. Stop by the 1926 Lacoochee School and give the school bell a ring. Check out the office of Irvin S. Futch, a turn-of-the-century dentist. Those instruments look scary! A trip to the Jack Bromley Shoe Repair Shop is good for the soul — not to mention the heel.

Other highlights

See the collections of Native American artifacts, quilts, pottery and musical instruments. Don't miss the amazing collection of dolls depicting Florida's First Ladies in their inaugural gowns. Be sure to check out the 1910 reconstructed citrus packing facility. And, at various times, visitors can watch the production of sugar cane syrup made at the Pioneer mill.

The facts

Pioneer Florida Museum & Village
15602 Pioneer Museum Road
Dade City, FL 33523
(352) 567-0262

Admission: $5 adults, $4 seniors 55 and older, $2 students 6 to 18, free for children 5 and younger.

Hours: Tuesday through Saturday 10 a.m. to 5 p.m.

www.pioneerfloridamuseum.org

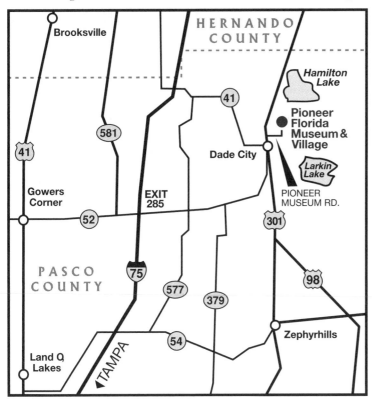

Directions

From Tampa, take Interstate 75 north to exit 285 (State Road 52) toward Dade City. Turn right on S.R. 52. Turn left onto U.S. 98 (Lakeland Road). Make a slight turn onto U.S. 301 north. Turn right onto Pioneer Museum Road.

Young and old Floridians alike will enjoy this look at old Florida.

Rogers' Christmas House & Village

jingle all the way!

From displays of collectibles to decorations, the five houses here are packed with Christmas cheer and unique gifts.

The trip

It's time to hop aboard the holiday express! January or December, or anytime in between, Rogers' Christmas House is a beautiful way to spend the holidays.

What to see

This village of five houses started as a gift shop in the early 1950s. Now you can buy everything from decorations to linens and gourmet food. Make sure you stroll through all of the houses and the gardens outside.

You might want to select an ornament by Christopher Radko, America's premier ornament designer. In fact, his ornaments can be seen on the White House Christmas tree every year. Also check out the 56 miniature houses — a favorite for dollhouse fans.

Other highlights

The concrete walkway is a tribute to patrons. Be sure to see who's been here before you.

The facts

Rogers' Christmas House & Village
103 S. Saxon Ave.
Brooksville, FL 34601
(352) 796-2415

Admission: *Free.*

Hours: *Daily 10 a.m. to 5 p.m.*
Closed Christmas, Easter, Thanksgiving.

www.rogerschristmashouse.com

Directions

From Tampa, take Interstate 75 north to the Brooksville/Ridge Manor exit 301 west to Brooksville. That road becomes U.S. 50 Alt. Follow it about 10 miles to Brooksville. Rogers' Christmas House Village will be on the right.

Christmas 365 days a year.

Ron Jon Surf Shop

not your father's surf shop

Ron Jon Surf Shop

The exterior of Ron Jon's flagship store pays tribute to the beach lifestyle through photos and sand sculptures. Inside, you'll find all the accessories you could need or want for a beach visit.

The trip

Head east from the Tampa Bay area, and you'll see the billboards. You can't miss them along Interstate 4 as you head to Cocoa Beach. It's called the "waterworld of eternal summer fun."

What to see

Need a T-shirt? At last count, they've sold more than 16 million "t's". Ron Jon also sells shorts, swim suits, shoes and skirts. And check out the skateboards and sunblock. Then there are the surfboards, skimboards and bodyboards. These folks are serious about their board knowledge. The place is huge! With 52,000 square feet, the store covers more than two acres. It's more of a palace than a surf shop. Visit once and you'll be hooked.

Other highlights

See the sculptures outside the store. They're larger than life and worth a look. Or shop at Ron Jon Watersports. Forget something? Ron Jon rents beach bikes and other sporting equipment. And, when you're tired after a hard day's ride, take a break at the Ron Jon Surf Grill at the Ron Jon Cape Caribe Resort just down the road at Jetty Park.

The facts

Ron Jon Surf Shop
4151 N. Atlantic Ave.
Cocoa Beach, FL 32931
(321) 799-8820

Admission: *Free.*

Hours: *24 hours a day, 365 days a year.*

www.ronjons.com

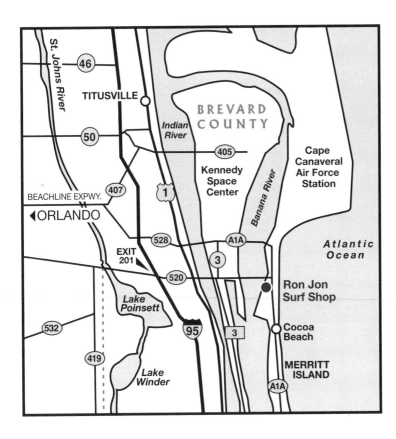

Directions

From Tampa, take Interstate 4 to Beachline Expressway (State Road 528) or State Road 520 to Cocoa Beach. Ron Jon is at the corner of S.R. 520 and A1A, about 1 minute from the Atlantic Ocean.

A surfing experience that has nothing to do with changing channels on TV.

Silver Springs

a Florida classic

Silver Springs

Glass bottom boats let passengers peer into the depths of the natural artesian springs. On dry land, you'll learn about the Florida panther in the Panther Prowl exhibit.

The trip

Florida's original attraction has been around since the 1870s and it's clear why — the crystal-clear spring water.

What to see

Since they were invented in 1878, the glass bottom boats of Silver Springs have fascinated millions. Looking down into the depths you can see the star of the show — the beautiful spring waters. These waters have been featured in a long list of movies and TV shows, including six "Tarzan" movies, two James Bond movies and the "Sea Hunt" TV show.

On a boat tour, you'll see the place where the monster emerged in the 1954 horror classic, "Creature from the Black Lagoon."

Other highlights

Wildlife exhibits are everywhere. Panther Prowl lets you see a true Florida panther. World of Bears is the largest exhibit of its kind in the world. And don't forget the Lost River Voyage and the 14 River Cruise. There's also a special spot for children: "Kids Ahoy! Playland" features a carousel, fishing games and a playground, all on a replica of an 1800s riverboat. Children also will love the Kritter Korral where they can pet miniature horses and pot bellied pigs.

The facts

Silver Springs
5656 E. Silver Springs Blvd.
Silver Springs, FL 34488
(352) 236-2121

Admission: *$33.99 for adults, $24.99 children 3 to 10, $30.99 seniors, free for children 2 and younger.*

Hours: *Daily in summer 10 a.m. to 5 p.m. From August 18 through the holidays, open Friday through Sunday.*

www.silversprings.com

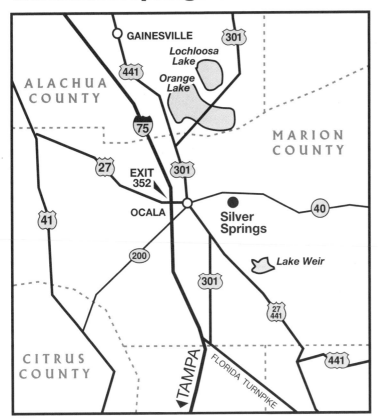

This is a full day's worth of fun.

Directions

From Tampa, take Interstate 75 to exit 352 (State Road 40) east 10 miles. Silver Springs will be on the right.

▼ **13**

Weeki Wachee Springs

mermaid mania

Passengers on the Wilderness River Cruise can observe herons, otters, raccoons, osprey and endangered wood storks along the Weeki Wachee River. Weeki Wachee's famous mermaids perform every day in the underwater theater.

Weeki Wachee Spring

The trip

Weeki Wachee, home of those famous mermaids, is one of Florida's oldest theme parks. Now, the 27-acre waterpark includes water slides and boat rides, in addition to an underwater production of "The Little Mermaid."

What to see

Have you ever tried drinking a soft drink while wearing skates — under water? Weeki Wachee Springs' famous mermaids have enchanted millions of visitors with their performances in the world's only underwater spring theater.

Other highlights

Another must-do is a trip along the enchanted river of the mermaids. Sit back and enjoy the natural beauty along the Weeki Wachee River. If thrills and spills are your speed, take the plunge into the spring water or zoom down the three-story waterslide.

The facts

Weeki Wachee Springs
6131 Commercial Way
Spring Hill, FL 34606
(352) 596-2062

Admission: $24.95 adults, $18.95 seniors, $16.95 children 3 to 10, free for ages 2 and younger. Prices adjusted seasonally from Labor Day through March.

Hours: Opens 10 a.m. daily. Closing times vary during summer and select holidays. Water park open seasonally. Call for daily schedule.

www.weekiwachee.com

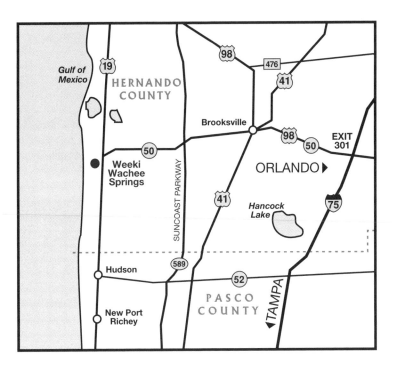

Directions

From Tampa, take Interstate 75 to exit 301 (State Road 50 west) about 20 miles to U.S.19. Weeki Wachee is at the intersection of U.S.19 and S.R. 50 in Hernando County.

An old-fashioned 'theme park,' a delightful day.

▼
14

DeLeon Springs
State Park

sweet dreams

The water here is 72 degrees, perfect for swimming from a boat or a bank. Or, take the Eco/History Boat Tour through Spring Garden Lake. The wildlife is abundant, the landscape, beautiful.

The trip

As long as 6,000 years ago, Native Americans utilized DeLeon Springs. In the early 1800s, settlers built sugar and cotton plants here, although the buildings were demolished during the Second Seminole War. The springs were rediscovered in the 1880s when promoters touted the locale as a winter resort complete with its own fountain of youth spouting "deliciously healthy" waters that tasted of soda and sulphur.

What to see

Swim in the warm waters or rent a canoe, kayak or paddleboat to explore the spring and spring run. DeLeon Springs flows into the Lake Woodruff National Wildlife Refuge where canoeists and kayakers can tour the 18,000 acres of lakes, creeks, and marshes. Sightseers can take the Eco/History Boat Tour — a 45-minute trip to Spring Garden Lake or one and a half hour trip to Lake Woodruff. Bring your binoculars to catch a glimpse of alligators, bald eagles and many species of wading birds found along the way.

Other highlights

At The Old Spanish Sugar Mill Grill and Griddle House, guests can make their delicious pancakes on their own personal griddle. And be sure to visit "Old Methuselah" — an enormous bald cypress tree said to be more than 500 years old. At the Visitor Center, enjoy exhibits on park history and DVD presentations on Florida's springs, the St. Johns River and the Everglades.

The facts

DeLeon Springs State Park
601 Ponce DeLeon Blvd.
DeLeon Springs, Florida 32130
(386) 985-4212

Admission: $5 per vehicle for up to 8 people.
$1 pavilion fee for pedestrians, bicyclists, extra passengers,
passengers in vehicles with holders of entrance permits.
Pavilion fees start at $30, plus tax, for a small one, and
$60, plus tax, for a large one.

Hours: Park open 8 a.m. until sundown daily.
Restaurant hours are Monday through Friday, 9 a.m. to
5 p.m. and Saturday, Sunday, 8 a.m. to 5 p.m., serving
until 4 p.m. Eco/History Boat Tour at 11 a.m. and 1 p.m.
daily. Tour reservations: (386) 837-5537.

www.floridastateparks.org/ deleonsprings

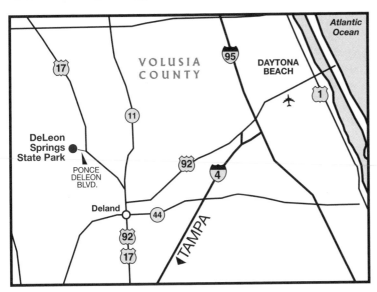

Directions

From Tampa, take Interstate 4 to U.S. 17. Take U.S. 17
north from Deland for approximately 6 miles, following the
State Park signs. Turn left onto Ponce DeLeon Blvd. then
travel approximately 1 mile to the entrance to DeLeon
Springs State Park.

Be sure to take time to enjoy the beautiful trails on your visit.

Historic Bok Sanctuary

majestic beauty

The 157 acres of Olmsted-designed landscape gardens include flowering plants such as azaleas and camellias, along with ferns, palms, oaks and pines. Left, the carillon houses 60 bronze bells.

Historic Bok Sanctuary

The trip

Before he came to America, Edward Bok got this advice from his grandmother: "Make you the world a bit better or more beautiful because you have lived in it." Years later, author, publisher and Pulitzer Prize winner Edward Bok did just that. This is truly a place of beauty, peace and reflection.

What to see

The tower is built on peninsular Florida's highest point: elevation 298 feet. The detailed carvings on the 205-foot singing tower depict Florida's flora and fauna. The impressive brass door, depicting the Biblical story of creation, is just one of the tower's architectural treasures.

Other highlights

The tower houses one of the world's greatest carillons, making this a place of joyful music. You'll also want to stop by Pinewood Estate, a Mediterranean mansion that's an example of an early Florida winter retreat. Stay at nearby Chalet Suzanne, a gourmet retreat with European-style rooms.

The facts

Historic Bok Sanctuary
1151 Tower Blvd.
Lake Wales, FL 33853
(863) 676-9412 *(Recorded Information)*
(863) 676-1408 *(Administrative Offices)*

Admission: *$10 adults, $3 children 5 to 12,*
free for children younger than 5.

Hours: *Daily 8 a.m. to 6 p.m. (last admission is*
5 p.m.). Carillon concerts daily at 1 and 3 p.m.

www.boksanctuary.org

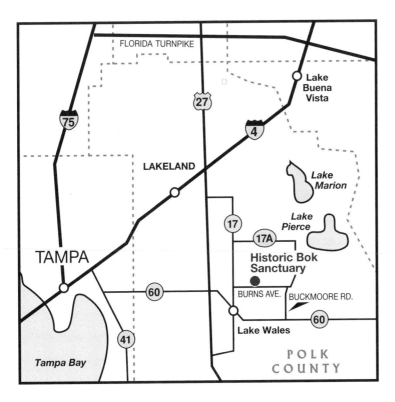

Beautiful sights, beautiful sounds in a beautiful Florida setting.

Directions

From Tampa, take State Road 60 east to Lake Wales. At Buckmoore Road in Lake Wales, turn left and go up the hill to the stop light, which is Burns Avenue. Turn left on Burns Avenue. Historic Bok Sanctuary is up the hill on the right.

Cypress Gardens Adventure Park

▼
16

bring the kids and grandparents

Florida Cypress Gardens Inc.

With multiple roller coasters and spectacular water skiing shows, Cypress Gardens has evolved into one of Florida's unique theme parks.

The trip

Enter a whole new world at Cypress Gardens Adventure Park. Established in 1936, this exquisite place is Florida's first theme park. It's still a stunning place to visit!

What to see

The Botanical Gardens are a tropical paradise. The topiaries are a delight. The Adventure Park now boasts 40 rides, including six coasters!

Other highlights

Cypress Gardens Adventure Park is called the "Water Ski Capital of the World," and no wonder. The shows are spectacular. Plan to get wet at Splash Island, a water park within a park, at no extra charge. Crash rolling waves, zip down a slide or just float along a lazy river.

The facts

Cypress Gardens Adventure Park
6000 Cypress Gardens Blvd.
Winter Haven, FL 33884
(863) 324-2111

Admission: *$39.95 children and adults 10 to 59, $34.95 children 3 to 9 and seniors 60 and older, free for children 2 and younger. Second day ticket is free.*

Hours: *Daily from 10 a.m. to 7 p.m. Closed Thanksgiving and Christmas.*

www.cypressgardens.com

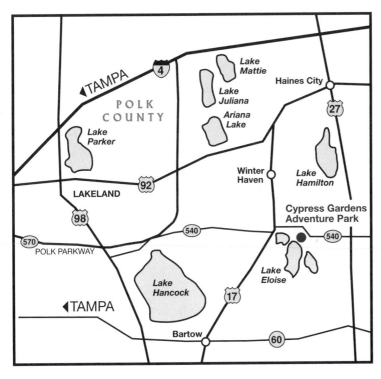

Directions

From Tampa, take Interstate 4 to Polk Parkway east. Exit State Road 540 east, Winter Lake Road. Follow to the end and turn left on Highway 17 north. Travel 2 miles over the bridge to first light. Turn right. Park is on the right at Kehoe Way.

If a picture is worth a thousand words, you'll need a few dictionaries for this place.

Cypress Gardens Adventure Park

The Florida Air Museum at Sun 'n Fun

17

enjoy this attraction on the fly

Planes of all shapes, sizes and designs fill the Florida Air Museum.

Florida Air Museum

The trip

Lakeland's annual Sun 'n Fun Fly-in is the perfect week for aviation fans. The other 51 weeks of the year, things are quieter here. But don't let that fool you. This museum offers plenty of aviation action.

What to see

This is a perfect place for aviation enthusiasts. Everywhere you turn, an airplane awaits. You can explore the homemade planes, ultralights, antique and classic planes and all types of aircraft engines. And the exhibit of military planes and memorabilia is fascinating.

Other highlights

You don't need to be a pilot to enjoy this museum. Special exhibits cater to all kinds of interests. Check out the collection of Charles Lindbergh memorabilia, the Howard Hughes archives and uniforms and mementos from the now-defunct National Airlines. There is also a retired U.S. Navy F-14 fighter "Tomcat" on display. During summer months, the museum offers aviation camp for children ages 8 and older.

The facts

The Florida Air Museum at Sun' n Fun
4175 Medulla Road
Lakeland, FL 33811
(863) 644-2431

Admission: *$8 adults, $6 seniors, $4 children 8 to 12, free for children 7 and younger.*

Hours: *Monday through Friday 9 a.m. to 5 p.m., Saturday 10 a.m. to 4 p.m., Sunday noon to 4 p.m. Closed on major holidays.*

www.floridaairmuseum.org

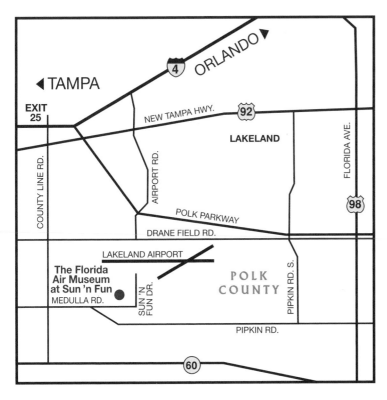

Directions

From Tampa, take Interstate 4 to exit 25 (County Line Road). Proceed south on County Line Road. Turn left (east) on W. Pipkin Road, make left to Medulla Road.

Sights and sounds to make your heart soar.

Spook Hill

what comes down goes up?

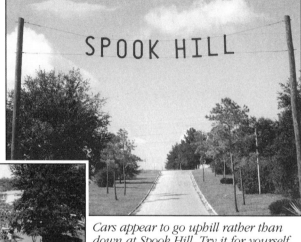

Cars appear to go uphill rather than down at Spook Hill. Try it for yourself.

The trip

They call it the mystery of Spook Hill where cars roll uphill. This is an inexpensive (make that free) trip for the entire family at a place that would make Newton think twice about his law of gravity.

What to see

The legend says that long ago an Indian chief fought with an alligator. The fight was ferocious. Day after day after day, the two battled. Finally the chief vanquished the gator. Some say the evil spirit of the alligator is behind the Spook Hill mischief. Others say the chief is protecting the city from the evil spirit of the alligator and Spook Hill is the result. Either way, cars still roll up the hill.

To try it, put your car in neutral at North Wales Drive at North Avenue. Release the brake and away you go. You'll have to drive it to believe it. But don't let it drive you mad!

Other highlights

Historic Bok Sanctuary, another **One Tank Trip**® destination, is nearby. You might want to visit both places the same day.

The facts

Lake Wales
Chamber of Commerce
340 W. Central Ave.
Lake Wales, FL 33859
(863) 676-3445

Admission: *Free.*

Hours: *Access to Spook Hill always open. Chamber hours 9 a.m. to 5 p.m. Monday through Friday.*

www.lakewaleschamber.com

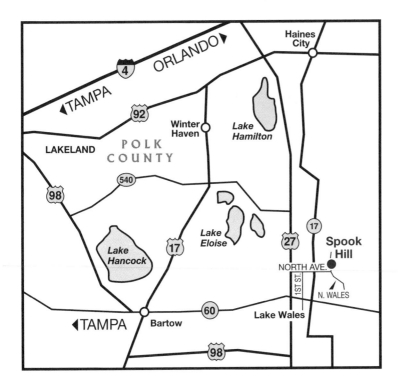

Directions

From Tampa, head east on State Road 60 to Lake Wales. Turn left at First Street (the first light) and follow it until it ends at North Avenue. Turn right on North Avenue and follow it until it ends on Wales Drive. Spook Hill is on Wales Drive.

Give it a try— if you dare...

Daytime Ybor City

afternoon delight!

▼
19

A view of a picturesque street in Ybor City, a designated National Historic Landmark. Below, the lavish entrance to the Centro Ybor complex.

This statue, located in Centro Ybor is of Don Vicente Martinez who built a thriving cigar business in the 1800s.

The trip

Mention Ybor City and some people think of the nightlife, calling it the Tampa Bay area's answer to Bourbon Street. But there's another Ybor City, and you can find it when the sun is out.

What to see

Famed Seventh Avenue offers all kinds of shopping, from specialty gift shops and home decorating, to LaTropicana, an authentic Cuban coffee shop. If you're hungry, try The Columbia Restaurant, which is run by the Gonzmart family. It's the largest and oldest Spanish restaurant in the U.S., and its flamenco show is one of the best in the country.

A walking map and guide is available at the visitors center to help you find all the sights.

Other highlights

Ybor City was once the cigar capital of the world. Today you can still see cigar rollers at work. Even if you don't smoke, you'll enjoy their living history lesson. And the Ybor City State Museum gives you a glimpse of Ybor's cigar industry in its heyday.

The facts

Ybor City Visitor's Information Center
1600 E. Eighth Ave.
Tampa, FL 33605
(813) 241-8838

Admission: *Visitor's Center is free. $3 to visit Ybor City State Museum.*

Hours: *Open daily, but call for hours at the museum. Restaurant and shop hours vary.*

www.ybor.org

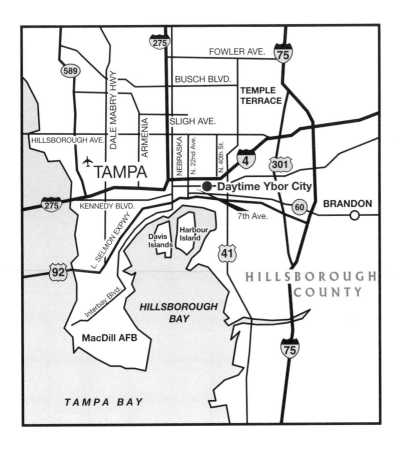

Make your visit a family affair or share the day with a special someone.

Directions

From Interstate 4, take 21st Street exit south to Seventh Avenue, the heart of Ybor City.

▼
20

Hillsborough River State Park

a camper's delight

The swinging bridge is just one way to explore the scenic beauty of Hillsborough River State Park.

The trip

The Hillsborough River is named for Wills Hill (1718-93), the Earl of Hillsborough. Set on 2,994 acres, this is one of Florida's oldest parks and one of the most breathtaking.

What to see

Whether in an R.V. or in a tent, the camping is great. You'll feel like you're in the woods, but with bathrooms and hot showers close by. Keep an eye out for the many raccoons and the occasional armadillo.

Other highlights

Rent a canoe and paddle up and down the river. You'll see turtles, all sorts of birds and perhaps an alligator or two. Hike one of the many trails, go fishing or take the plunge in the enormous half-acre swimming pool.

The facts

Hillsborough River State Park
15402 U.S. 301 N.
Thonotosassa, FL 33592
(813) 987-6771

Admission: *$4 per vehicle (limit 8 people) or $3 for one person. Swimming is $2 per person ages 6 and older, free 5 and younger. Call for camping rates.*

Hours: *Daily 8 a.m. to sundown; until 10 p.m. Fridays and Saturdays for arriving campers.*

www.dep.state.fl.us/parks

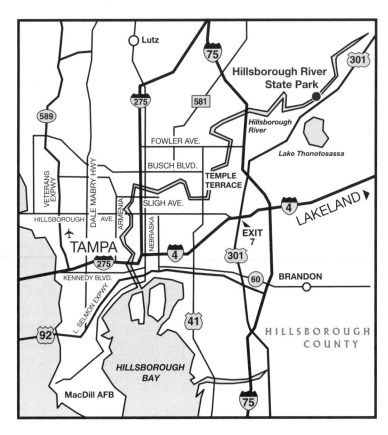

Directions
From Interstate 4 take exit 7 to U.S. 301 north. The park is 14 miles down the road on the left.

Camp in comfort at this exceptional state park.

▼
21

Tampa's Lowry Park Zoo

this place is a real zoo!

Two visitors get up close and personal with this friendly giraffe. This massive African elephant creates his own splash zone. It's a great way to get through a steamy day.

Lowry Park Zoo

The trip

If you haven't been to the zoo in a while, or ever, stop by. Every visit to this special place is an adventure. The zoo has a wonderful commitment to threatened and endangered species that shows in all of its programs.

What to see

The list of things to do, enjoy and learn is endless. There are more than 2,000 animals in lush natural habitats spread over 56 acres. Don't miss the Florida Manatee and Aquatic Center. You'll get a close-up look at Florida's beloved sea mammals. Check out the herd of African elephants that live in a savanna in the Safari Africa habitat area. And be sure to visit Buddy. He's a sloth bear and a pretty remarkable creature.

Other highlights

The wildlife shows are spectacular. Here's your chance to get personal with owls and eagles, lizards and frogs. And then there are the fountains. Billabong Fountain at Wallaroo Station is a kid favorite and a first rate splash zone. Jumping in and around the water is part of the zoo tradition.

The facts

Tampa's Lowry Park Zoo
1101 W. Sligh Ave.
Tampa, FL 33604
(813) 935-8552

Admission: *$18.95 children and adults 12 to 59, $17.95 seniors 60 and older, $14.50 children 3 to 11, free for children 2 and younger.*

Hours: *Daily 9:30 a.m. to 5 p.m. Closed Thanksgiving and Christmas.*

www.lowryparkzoo.com

This place brings out the animal... actually lots of animals.

Directions

From Interstate 275 in Tampa, take the Sligh Avenue exit 48 west and follow the signs to the Zoo (about 1 mile).

The Florida Aquarium

life down under

The 152,000-square-foot aquarium tells the story of water in Florida.

The Florida Aquarium

The trip

Since March 1995, the aquarium has been telling the story of water and its inhabitants — from wetlands to coral reefs, bays to beaches.

What to see

The Florida Aquarium, home to more than 20,000 aquatic plants and marine animals selected from Florida and around the world, is the cornerstone of the exhibits here. The Aquarium tells the story of water's journey to the sea beginning with a single drop of rain and its path through wetlands into bays and beaches, traveling into the coral reef and finally into the deep waters where the ocean's top predators are found.

Other highlights

Along the way, see river otters, alligators, stingrays and sharks! Visitors can immerse themselves in interactive programs such as Swim With The Fish and Dive With The Sharks where coming face-to-face with a 200-pound Goliath grouper is commonplace. Children can enjoy Explore A Shore, a 2.2-acre water adventure park with a 15-foot water-spouting eel! And forget the acrylic windows! Get up close and personal with African Black-footed Penguins in the "no borders, no barricades" Penguin Promenade daily at 10 a.m. and 3 p.m.

The facts

The Florida Aquarium
701 Channelside Drive
Tampa, FL 33602
(813) 273-4000

Admission: *$17.95 adults, $14.95 seniors 60 and older, $12.95 children 3 to 11, free for children younger than 3.*

Hours: *Daily 9:30 a.m. to 5 p.m. Closed Thanksgiving and Christmas.*

www.flaquarium.org

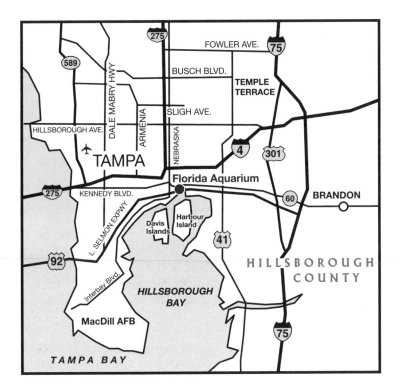

Directions

From Interstate 275, take exit 45-A Downtown East (Jefferson Street). Continue straight on Jefferson to Twiggs. Turn left to Channelside Drive. Turn right on Channelside Drive to Washington Street. Turn left on Washington Street to Aquarium Parking.

Talk to real sea explorers about Florida's aquatic world.

Bill Jackson Shop for Adventure

the only one of its kind

From camping to kayaking and beyond, Bill Jackson offers equipment for any outdoor adventure.

J. LaFray

The trip

Just a stone's throw from the very busy U.S. 19 in Pinellas Park, tucked away on five acres, is Bill Jackson's — Bill Jackson Shop for Adventure, to be exact — and the adventure is yours for the choosing. For more than half a century, a lot of folks have made this their destination for fun.

What to see

Want to learn to scuba dive? Learn in the 10-foot-deep indoor pool. Skiing? Hit the indoor slopes. There are almost 25,000 square feet of sporting equipment.

Don't worry if you have questions. "Mr. J" insists that the person who helps you is very active in that sport or activity.

Other highlights

Kayaks and canoes come in all shapes, sizes and colors. If you're more interested in fly fishing or archery, they've got just the thing.

The facts

Bill Jackson Shop for Adventure
9501 U.S. 19 N.
Pinellas Park, FL 33782
(727) 576-4169

Admission: *Free.*

Hours: *Monday through Friday 10 a.m. to 9 p.m.,
Saturday 10 a.m. to 6 p.m., Sunday 10 a.m. to 5 p.m.
Closed on major holidays.*

www.billjacksons.com

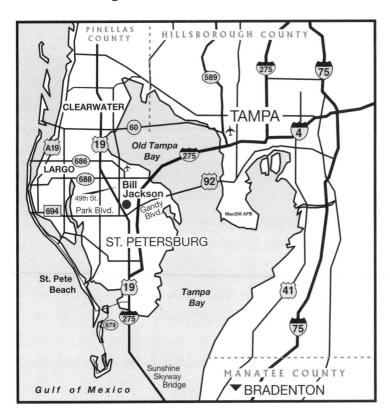

Directions

From Tampa, take Interstate 275 south, merge onto
Gandy Boulevard (State Road 694) toward Pinellas Park.
Merge onto U.S. 19 north toward Clearwater. Bill
Jackson's is just south of 49th Street.

Plan to spend at least an hour here. The people really know what they're talking about. How refreshing!

Boyd Hill
Nature Preserve

birding paradise

*Visitors can explore the natural beauty
of this park strolling along the miles of
trails and boardwalks.*

The trip

They call this place "St. Petersburg's Precious Wonder." It's amazing more people don't know about the 245-acre Boyd Hill Nature Preserve. Spend just a few minutes here and that "peaceful feeling" will embrace you.

What to see

This unspoiled setting offers more than three miles of trails and boardwalks. You'll see alligators, herons, gopher tortoises and more among the hardwood hammocks, sand pine scrub, pine flatwoods and willow marsh. Or just close your eyes and listen to the crickets, cicadas, woodpeckers and bees.

Other highlights

Be sure to see the work of metal sculptor Paul Eppling. At Wax Myrtle Pond you'll find two adventurous armadillos. And two dragon-like creatures guard the park. "Narcissus" lurks at the edge of the pond near the picnic area. "Tree Dragon" or "Forest Mentor" perches on a limb at the rear entrance of the nature center. Don't miss The Ripple Effect at the Lake Maggiore Environmental Education Center. It's a dynamic interactive exhibit showcasing Boyd Hill's distinct ecosystems that reveals how every action has an equal or greater reaction in the environment. Bring your camera, your bicycle, if you like, and the hot dogs! There's a picnic area with grills and sheltered tables.

The facts

Boyd Hill Nature Preserve
1101 Country Club Way South
St. Petersburg, FL 33705
(727) 893-7326

Admission: *$3 adults, $1.50 children 3 to 16, free for children younger than 3.*

Hours: *Tuesday through Thursday 9 a.m. to 8 p.m., Friday, Saturday 9 a.m. to 6 p.m., Sunday 11 a.m. to 6 p.m. Trails close a half hour before dusk. Closed Mondays, Thanksgiving, Christmas and New Year's Day.*

www.stpete.org/boyd

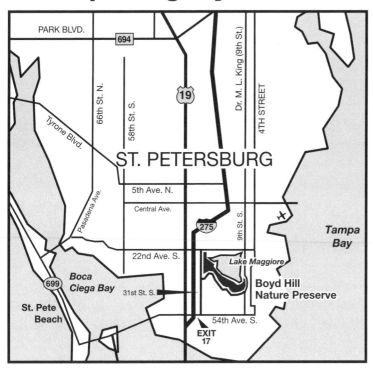

Directions

From Tampa, take Interstate 275 south to exit 17. Turn east onto 54th Ave. South. Turn left onto Dr. Martin Luther King Jr. Street South (9th Street South). Country Club Way South is four blocks on the left at the light. Park entrance is on the right.

Fresh air, wildlife, historical architecture and a peaceful oasis in busy St. Petersburg.

J. LaFray

Captain Memo's Pirate Cruise

go yo-ho!

A seaboard wedding onboard a custom designed pirate ship built to U.S. Coast Guard requirements in 1993.

Captain Memo's Pirate Cruise

The trip

Think pirates live only in history books? Here's a pirate ship, the "Pirate's Ransom," cleverly hidden away at the Clearwater Beach Marina where fun loving brigands offer friendly pirate pleasures.

What to see

To join a pirate cruise you need to get into character. Captain Memo's crew will get you fitted for hats and eye patches. Then it's time to sail the Gulf in search of pirate adventure. There are treasure hunts and pirate stories, games and songs, plus the occasional cannon fire.

Other highlights

The spirited crew will help keep you in the mood for adventure on your two-hour cruise. They'll also help you find dolphins that can be plentiful in the warm Gulf waters. In addition to the daytime cruises, Captain Memo offers champagne cruises, private charters, bay cruises, wedding services and children's birthday parties.

The facts

Captain Memo's Pirate Cruise
25 Causeway Blvd.,
Clearwater Marina, No. 3
Clearwater Beach, FL 33767
(727) 446-2587

Admission: *Call for rates for various cruises.*

Hours: *Daytime cruises depart at 10 a.m. and 2 p.m. year-round. Additional daily cruises are available from February through September. Call for departures for sunset champagne cruises or special events.*

www.captainmemo.com

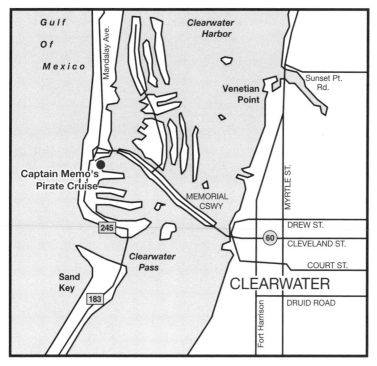

Directions

From Tampa, take the Courtney Campbell Causeway (Rt. 60) west to Memorial Causeway to Clearwater Beach. Cross the bridge, staying in the left hand lane. Take the 4th exit out of the traffic circle into the marina. Metered parking is available in the Marina.

Ahoy there mateys, this cruise is non-stop fun!

26

Clearwater Marine Aquarium

a great stop on the way to the beach

Clearwater Marine Aquarium

Winter, the remarkable dolphin outfitted with an artificial tail, swims at the Clearwater Aquarium where she has become a star.

The trip

No doubt many of us have quickly passed the sign. The Clearwater Aquarium sits right off the causeway to Clearwater Beach. In the last 25 years, it has been known as Sea-O-Rama, the Clearwater Marine Science Center, even the Florida Marine Aquarium.

What to see

The Marine Mammal Department offers educational programs that provide a behind-the-scenes look at dolphin and river otter care and conservation. "Day With a Dolphin" is designed for children ages 8 to 11, who are interested in learning more about dolphins and how they are trained. "Dolphin Encounter" is a 30-minute program for all ages that offers the opportunity to get a private behind-the-scenes look at the aquarium's resident bottlenose dolphins.

Don't miss Winter, the famous dolphin who lost her tail in an accident, but now is healthy and swims freely.

Other highlights

In addition to CMA's Atlantic bottlenose dolphins, there are also several species of sea turtle, North American river otters, brown pelicans, raccoons, opossums and others.

The facts

Clearwater Marine Aquarium
249 Windward Passage
Clearwater, FL 33767
(727) 441-1790
Toll free: (888) 239-9414

Admission: *$11 adults, $9 seniors 60 and older, $7.50 children 3 to 12.*

Hours: *Open Monday through Thursday 9 a.m. to 5 p.m., Friday, Saturday 9 a.m. to 9 p.m., Sunday 10 a.m. to 5 p.m.*
Closed Thanksgiving, Christmas, and New Year's Day.

www.seewinter.com

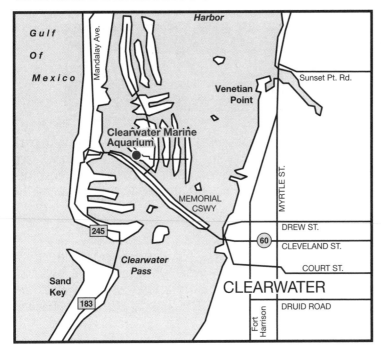

Directions

From Tampa, take State Road 60 in Pinellas County (Gulf-to-Bay Boulevard) west to Memorial Causeway. Follow signs to the Aquarium or follow the causeway to the light at Island Way. Turn right and then left at the single flashing light, which is Windward Passage. The aquarium is on the left.

This is truly a remarkable place where education, rescue and rehabilitation are of primary importance.

Fort De Soto Park

a bay area jewel

St. Petersburg-Clearwater

The opportunities to explore are endless at Fort De Soto. Learn about the history of the fort. Or take a break from your hectic routine and stroll or fish along one of the piers.

The trip

They call it Pinellas County's most diversified park. Set on five keys, the park includes 1,136 acres with protected plants and wildlife and miles of beach and fishing piers. Throw in a history lesson at the fort, and there's something for everyone here — canoes, kayaks, bike rentals to name some of the options.

What to see

To start, there's Fort De Soto. The first construction began in 1898. It was used as a military post until 1923. When you explore the layout of the fort and its guns, you can't help but learn a little history. Make sure you take the stairs to the top of the fort. The view of the Gulf water and beaches is spectacular.

Other highlights

The 1,000-foot Gulf Pier and 500-foot Bay Pier are wonders for those who fish, and 238 campsites are available for the adventurous. The 4 mile recreation trail is perfect for keeping in shape. Sun and surf lovers will enjoy the 7 miles of Fort De Soto waterfront. There is also a dog park with beach access. Finish with a cool drink at the snack bar; it doesn't get any better than this.

The facts

Fort De Soto Park
3500 Pinellas Bayway S.
Tierra Verde, FL 33715
(727) 866-2484 *(Park Patrol and Administration)*
(727) 582-2267 *(Camp Office)*

Admission: *Free, although there are two tolls before you get to the park. Call for campsite information and rates. Reservations can be made online, in person or by telephone.*

Hours: *Daily from 7 a.m. until dusk. The camp office is open daily from 8 a.m. to 9 p.m.*

www.pinellascounty.org/park

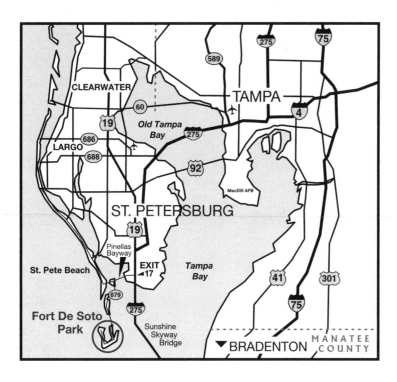

Try one of the campsites on the water. Simply perfect.

Directions
From Tampa, take Interstate 275 south to exit 17 west. Turn left at the light onto State Road 679, which will lead you directly to the park.

Gulfport Gallery Walk

a wonderful little secret

This whimsical sign greets visitors to Gulfport Artist Village, a lively artist colony that hosts a twice-a-month exposition.

The trip

Only 10 minutes from the Gulf beaches and 15 minutes from downtown St. Petersburg is the quaint and cozy setting of Gulfport. Every month they burn the midnight oil so you can stroll among the displays of works by local artists.

What to see

On the first Friday night of the month and third Saturday night, artists in the Gulfport Art Village display their works for one and all to see. Like paintings? There are plenty of styles to enjoy. How about glass work? Here is the kind of stuff that will fire you up and blow you away. You'll also see hand-thrown pottery, handmade jewelry and fine photography.

Other highlights

As you stroll among the booths and shops, local musicians will entertain you. Most shops serve free refreshments, including wine and cheese. And when you get tired of walking you can catch a free ride on the city trolley.

The facts

Gulfport Gallery Walk
Gulfport Chamber of Commerce
Bank of America Building
2808 58th St.
(727) 344-3711

Admission: *Free.*

Hours: *The Gallery Walk is from 6 p.m. to 10 p.m. on the first Friday evening of the month. The Saturday Stroll is from 6 p.m. to 10 p.m. on the third Saturday of the month.*

www.gulfportchamberofcommerce.com

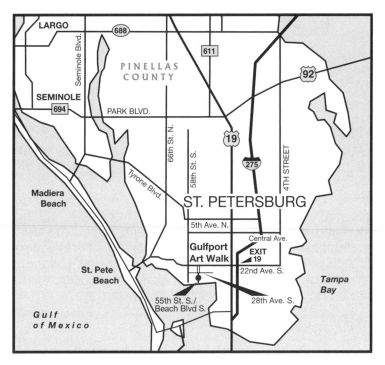

Directions

From Tampa, take Interstate 275 south to exit 19. Head west on 22nd Avenue South. Drive about 2 miles to Beach Boulevard South (55th Street South) and turn left. The Gulfport Art Village is south of 28th Avenue South on Beach Boulevard (55th Street) in Historic Gulfport.

The Friday Night Walk is a perfect way to kick off the weekend!

Haslam's Bookstore

simply a treasure

Haslam's started as a used bookstore, but over the years it grew to be Florida's largest new and used bookstore. Just roaming the stacks is a day's occupation.

J. LaFray

The trip

Haslam's calls itself "Florida's greatest rainy-day attraction!" But it certainly doesn't have to be a rainy day to stop by and browse among the 300,000 books.

What to see

Haslam's is the largest independently owned bookstore in the Southeast. Owned and operated by Ray and Suzanne Hinst, the store has offered new and used books that cater to all kinds of interests since 1933. There is a huge selection of fiction, nonfiction and children's books. Even if you're not sure what you're looking for, stroll among the rows and rows of books. Something's sure to catch your eye.

Other highlights

Haslam's even has its resident ghost, and a literary ghost at that. Jack Kerouac lived in St. Petersburg for a while and would come to Haslam's to rearrange his books so they would sell better. Now, even though he's dead, some believe his ghost is still rearranging.

After your visit here, stop by other attractions in lovely downtown St. Petersburg, including The Pier, the Museum of Fine Arts, the Salvador Dali Museum, and the Renaissance Vinoy Resort.

The facts

Haslam's Bookstore
2025 Central Ave.
St. Petersburg, FL 33713
(727) 822-8616

Admission: *Free.*

Hours: *Monday to Saturday 10 a.m. to 6:30 p.m.*
Closed Sundays.

www.haslams.com

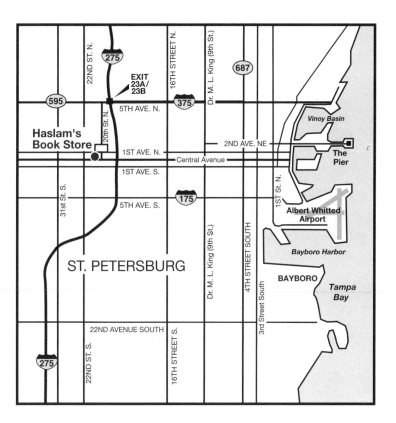

Directions

From Tampa, drive south on Interstate 275 and take exit 23-B to 20th Street. Head south on 20th Street and turn right on Central Avenue. Driving north on Interstate 275, take exit 23-A and turn right on Ninth Street, and again on Central.

Haslam's is a step into the past that you won't want to miss.

Heritage Village

a blast from the past

A re-enactor helps bring history alive at the 21-acre living history museum. Your walk through history at Heritage Village will include a stop by Heritage Mercantile and the House of Seven Gables, a 13-room Victorian building.

The trip

Nestled among the pine and palmetto in Largo sits a slice of Florida's past. Explore history at Heritage Village, a collection of more than 20 buildings that serve as a remarkable reminder of the state's rich background.

What to see

You can start with the McMullen-Coachman Loghouse. Built in the 1850s, this house is the oldest existing structure in Pinellas County. And it still rocks! Sit a spell in one of the rocking chairs on the front porch and let history speak to you. Or begin at the H. C. Smith Store. Not only is the store stocked with goods, there's also a garage and a barbershop full of the stuff of memories.

Other highlights

Among the buildings and museum, you'll be sure to find something that will capture the imagination of every member of your family. There's the House of Seven Gables, a Victorian home; the Harris School, a reproduction of a 1912 one-room schoolhouse; the La France Fire Engine, the first modern fire engine used in Belleair; and the Sulphur Springs Depot and Caboose, a wonderful railroad museum.

The facts

Heritage Village
11909 125th St. N.
Largo, FL 33774
(727) 582-2123

Admission: *Free, but donations accepted.*

Hours: *Tuesday through Saturday 10 a.m. to 4 p.m., Sunday 1 p.m. to 4 p.m. Closed Mondays and major holidays.*

www.pinellascounty.org/heritage

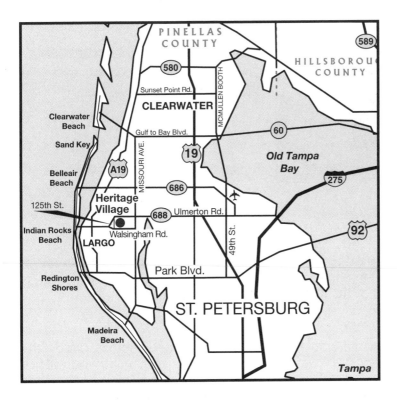

Directions

From Tampa, take Interstate 275 south to exit 31 (Ulmerton Road/State Road 688) west to 125th Street. Turn left on 121st Avenue, then right on 125th Street. Go past the County Extension Service to Gate 1 at Heritage Village.

A remarkable reminder of Florida's rich background.

Museum of Fine Arts

up close with the masters

J. LaFray

"Poppy" by Georgia O'Keefe, is part of the fine art collection on view in the 20 galleries at the Museum of Fine Arts.

The trip

You'll find a treasure, make that *treasures*, beautifully tucked away in downtown St. Petersburg. The Museum of Fine Arts, opened in 1965, is considered one of the finest museums in the Southeast.

What to see

You'll learn that the French artist Pierre Auguste Renoir is called "the painter of the joy of living." In his works on display here, you will see why. Other French artists in the collection include Claude Monet, Paul Cézanne and Auguste Rodin. You'll also see American works, including the brilliant "Poppy" by Georgia O'Keefe.

Other highlights

The building, with a newly added wing, is worth a trip, with its beautiful design and exquisite gardens. Sip a glass of wine in the museum cafe or stroll through the Sculpture Gardens for a unique experience.

The facts

Museum of Fine Arts
255 Beach Drive N.E.
St. Petersburg, FL 33701
(727) 896-2667

Admission: *$12 adults, $10 seniors 65 and older, $6 college students with current IDs, $6 children 7 to 18, free for children 6 and younger.*

Hours: *Tuesday through Saturday 10 a.m. to 5 p.m., Sunday 1 p.m. to 5 p.m.*
Closed Mondays, New Year's Day, Martin Luther King Day, Independence Day, Thanksgiving and Christmas.

www.fine-arts.org

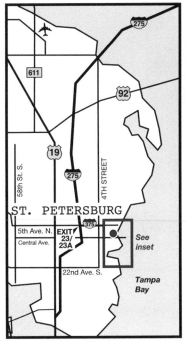

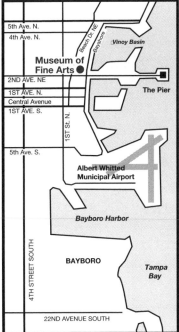

Directions

From Tampa, take Interstate 275 south to exit 23-A southbound or 23 northbound. Look for signs for The Pier. Continue straight until the road ends at Beach Drive; make a right on Beach Drive and the museum is past the park on the left side.

Whether you're an art lover or just curious, a memorable experience awaits.

Pass-a-Grille

a superb seaside getaway

The captivating beach and warm Gulf waters on Pass-a-Grille beckon to visitors.

The trip

At the tip of Pinellas County, you'll find a superb seaside destination. And there's no extra charge for the sun, surf, sand and shells.

What to see

History books will tell you Pass-a-Grille was the first established town on the barrier islands of Florida's west coast. But it's also a relaxing place for a day, a week or forever on the beach. This is the perfect spot to dip your toes in the warm Gulf water and stay awhile.

Parking is easier to find here than at most area beaches. But keep those quarters handy. Tickets happen.

Other highlights

Evander Preston's elegant jewelry shop, with exquisite handcrafted gold, offers much for the discriminating shopper. And beachside concessions offer gastronomic delights to enjoy while watching the sunset. Visit the Seahorse Grill by the Gulf for an early morning breakfast of fresh fruit.

The facts

Tampa Bay Beaches
Chamber of Commerce
St. Pete Beach Office
6990 Gulf Blvd.
St. Pete Beach, FL 33706
(727) 360-6957
Toll free: (800) 944-1847

Admission: *Free.*

Hours: *The beach is always open. Store and restaurant hours vary, so check ahead.*

www.tampabaybeaches.com

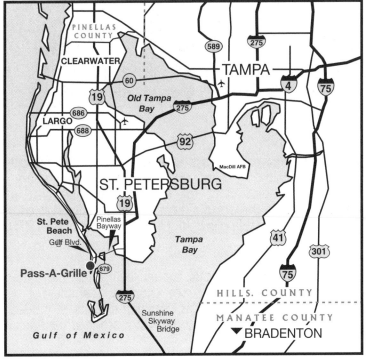

Directions

From Tampa, take Interstate 275 south to the St. Pete Beach exit (Pinellas Bayway) west until the bayway stops at the Don CeSar hotel. Turn left onto Gulf Boulevard and follow it to the end, then turn right to the beach.

One of Pinellas County's most coveted beach spots.

Salvador Dali Museum

hello, Dali!

Salvador Dali Museum

"The Disintegration of the Persistence of Memory," above and the "Hallucinogenic Toreador," right, are two of the bewildering and beautiful paintings by surrealist Salvador Dali on display at the museum.

The trip

The striking, often bizarre images of artist Salvador Dali are dramatically displayed at this extraordinary museum set alongside St. Petersburg's beautiful Bayboro Harbor. Dedicated to the leader of the Surrealist art movement, the museum houses the world's most comprehensive collection of Dali's works with especially notable oils dating from 1917 through 1970.

What to see

For the true art lover, or just for the curious, the museum offers more than galleries of Dali's famous paintings. You'll see exquisite examples of his sculptures, holograms and art glass as well as changing exhibits of modern artists who reflect Dali's quest to examine the deepest reaches of the human mind.

Other highlights

The gift shop is filled with exotic and sometimes eccentric items. T-shirts with Dali designs, sure, but also stunning jewelry, watches, fragrances and unusual games and toys for children. Check the on-line calendar for Saturday morning hands-on events for families or monthly coffee gatherings with the curator.

The facts

Salvador Dali Museum
1000 Third St. S.
St. Petersburg, FL 33701
(727) 823-3767

Admission: *$15 adults, $13.50 seniors, $10 students with current IDs (children 11 and older), $4 children 5 to 9, free for children 4 and younger. Admission $5 after 5 p.m. on Thursdays.*

Hours: *Monday, Tuesday, Wednesday and Saturday from 9:30 a.m. to 5:30 p.m., Friday 9:30 a.m. to 6:30 p.m., Sundays noon to 5:30 p.m. Closed Thanksgiving and Christmas.*

www.salvadordalimuseum.org

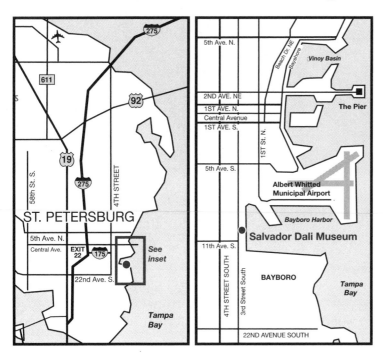

Directions

From Tampa, take Interstate 275 south to exit 22 (Interstate 175 east) towards Tropicana Field (exit will be on your left). Follow until end. Take a right onto Third Street South. Continue a half mile. Museum will be on the left.

The galleries offer a mind-bending experience.

Sawgrass Lake Park

mother nature on display

Explore the natural beauty of Pinellas County at this scenic park.

The trip

Here, in Florida's most densely populated county, sits a remarkable 400-acre park of wildlife and natural beauty.

What to see

This is one of Florida's best-kept secrets. Get out your binoculars and marvel at the variety of wildlife. You'll see alligators, blue heron, osprey, soft-shell turtles, wood stork and a turkey vulture or two.

Other highlights

More than a mile of scenic boardwalk and an observation tower let you get as close to — or as far from — nature as you want. Bring a picnic, but be aware that seating at the picnic shelter is on a first-come-first-serve basis. You can sit at one of the shelters and let nature serenade you with the sights and sounds of this lush environment.

The facts

Sawgrass Lake Park
7400 25th St. N.
St. Petersburg, FL 33702
(727) 217-7256

Admission: *Free.*

Hours: *Daily 7 a.m. to dusk.*

www.pinellascounty.org/park/16
_Sawgrass.htm

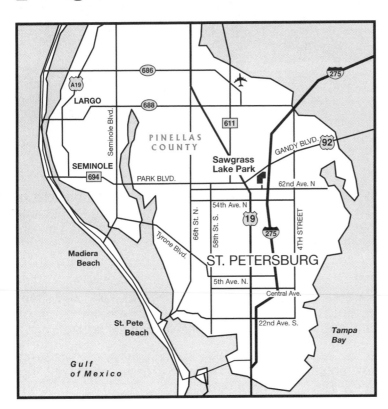

Directions

From Tampa, take Interstate 275 to exit 28 (Gandy Blvd.) and head west to U.S. 19. Continue south on U.S. 19 to 62nd Avenue North. Head east on 62nd Ave. N. to 25th Street. Turn left on 25th Street to reach the park.

At every turn, a wonder for the eyes.

Tarpon Springs

bring your appetite

Sponge boats and diving are part of the history of Tarpon Springs

Tarpon Springs Chamber of Commerce

St. Petersburg Clearwater Convention Bureau

The trip

Just 30 minutes north of Tampa-St. Petersburg is the enchanting city of Tarpon Springs, a city that is so many things. Greeks began immigrating to Tarpon Springs in 1906 to work in the sponge industry, and they are still here more than a century later.

What to see

Sponges from Tarpon Springs come in all shapes and sizes, and shops along the sponge docks offer quite a variety. You can even take a tour on a sponge boat and watch a diver demonstrate sponge harvesting.

If food is something you like, you've come to the right place. The gyros and octopus are mouth-watering. But why save dessert for last? The baklava is to die for. Hellas is a favorite bakery.

Other highlights

St. Nicholas Greek Orthodox Cathedral, a monument of love, faith and devotion, is truly magnificent. The church is the center of the Epiphany celebration on January 6 every year. The celebration includes the Greek Cross Ceremony, where young men dive for a white cross thrown into Spring Bayou. The diver who retrieves the cross is considered to be blessed with good luck for a year.

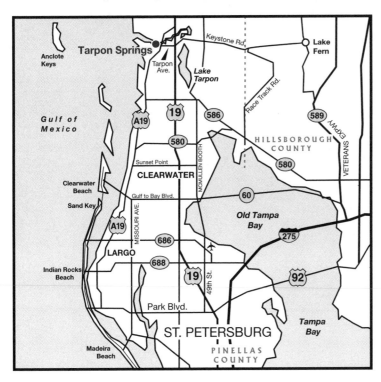
The facts

Tarpon Springs
Chamber of Commerce
11 E. Orange St.
Tarpon Springs, FL 34689
(727) 937-6109

Admission: *Free.*

Hours: *Restaurant and shop hours vary.*

www.tarponsprings.com

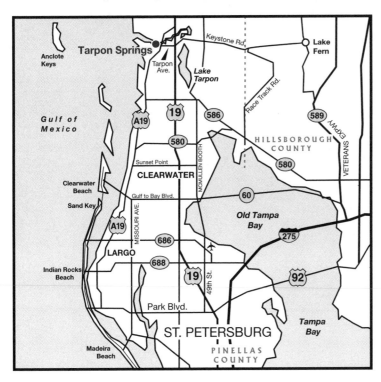

Directions

From Tampa, take Interstate 275 south to exit 31 (Ulmerton Road/State Road 688) west to U.S.19. Head north on U.S.19 and take Tarpon Avenue west to Tarpon Springs. Turn right at Alt. U.S. 19 (Pinellas Avenue) and head north. Turn left at Dodecanese Boulevard, which will take you to the sponge dock district. Street parking is limited, but there are lots along Dodecanese.

Make like a sponge and soak up the atmosphere.

Ted Peters
Famous Smoked Fish

talk about good taste!

Mullet, mackerel, and salmon smoked to perfection, are the specialties at this landmark restaurant.

The trip

There's something fishy going on around here. For the most part, you can blame Ted Peters. For 50 years his landmark restaurant has been smoking. Literally!

What to see

Ted's smoker keeps busy. You can order any kind of fish you want, as long as it's mullet, mackerel, mahi-mahi or salmon. They've all been smoked for at least four to five hours in red oak. Add a serving of the restaurant's awesome German-style potato salad, and it's heaven. The indoor-outdoor restaurant has served more than 100,000 pounds of fish a year for years. Dine inside or alfresco on the breezy patio.

Other highlights

The menu's a simple one. An item is considered "new" if it's been on the menu for less than 10 years. And if you're not in the mood for fish, they serve a killer burger.

The facts

Ted Peters Famous Smoked Fish
1350 Pasadena Ave. S.
St. Petersburg, FL 33707
(727) 381-7931

Admission: Free.

Hours: *Wednesday through Monday 11:30 a.m. to 7:30 p.m. Closed Tuesdays. Closed Thanksgiving and Christmas.*

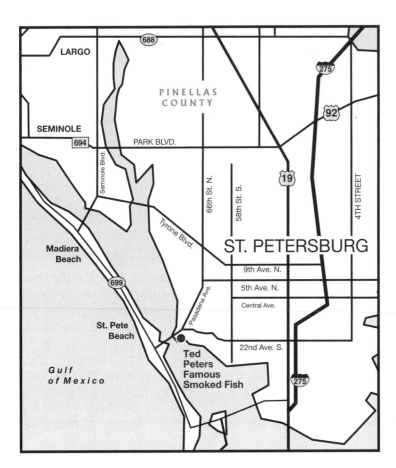

Directions

From Tampa, take Interstate 275 south to the Fifth Avenue North exit west to 66th Street. Turn left on 66th Street. It becomes Pasadena Avenue.

Smoking, at least over red oak, is permitted.

The Pier

a St. Petersburg treasure

Nestled in the waters of Tampa Bay along the St. Petersburg waterfront, The Pier offers a variety of shopping and dining.

The trip

For some, The Pier is a place to drop a fishing line and hope for the best. For others, it's shop 'til you drop. Either way, this upside-down pyramid, all five stories of it, offers plenty to see and do.

What to see

If shopping is your bag, you can fill it here. Clothing and specialty food shops line the first floor of The Pier. If you'd rather be outside, bring your fishing pole and cast your line from the 2,400-foot pier that extends into Tampa Bay. On the second floor, at The Pier Aquarium, discover the fun of the interactive Fresh Fish Theater featuring sea creatures from around the world.

Other highlights

Grab a snack downstairs in the food court. Or head for one of the mouth-watering restaurants including Spanish cuisine at The Columbia Restaurant and island-style cuisine at Cha-Cha Coconuts Tropical Bar & Grill. Check out the friendly pier-loving pelicans.

The facts

The Pier
800 Second Ave. N.E.
St. Petersburg, FL 33701
(727) 821-6443

Admission: *Free.*

Hours: *Daily 10 a.m., Sunday 11 a.m. The aquarium is open Monday to Saturday 10 a.m. to 8 p.m., Sunday noon to 6 p.m. Restaurant hours vary.*

www.stpetepier.com

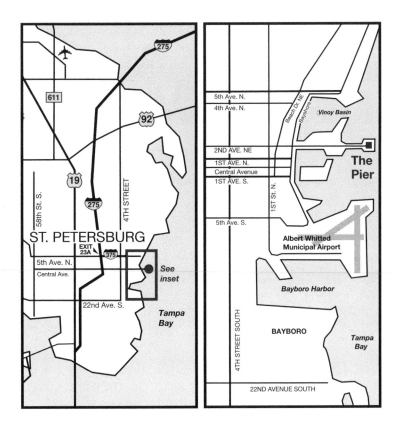

Directions

From Tampa, take Interstate 275 south to exit 23-A east and follow Fourth Avenue North to Beach Drive. Turn south to Second Avenue N.E. The Pier is at the east end of Second Avenue.

Fabulous shopping, great dining, wonderous views.

Gamble Plantation State Historic Park

a heaven for history buffs

Gamble Plantation State Historic Site

The mansion at the Gamble Plantation is the only antebellum plantation house surviving in south Florida.

The trip

One of southwest Florida's first settlers built this sugar plantation next to the Manatee River in Ellenton. Today, it's a living history lesson for visitors.

What to see

In the mid-1800s, Major Robert Gamble built one of the most successful sugar plantations in Florida. His mansion reflected his success. It was one of the finest homes on Florida's southwest coast. On your tour of the mansion, you'll see the house furnished in 19th-century style, depicting the lavish scale of the operation.

Even the mansion's construction is a history lesson. Two-foot-wide walls kept residents cool in the summer and offered protection from hurricanes. And a "dogtrot" separated the north section from the main building.

Other highlights

The mansion also played a role in the history of the Civil War. Confederate Secretary of State Judah P. Benjamin hid at the mansion after the fall of the Confederacy in 1865. From here, he fled to England. Today the mansion marks his famous escape.

The facts

Gamble Plantation State Historic Park
3708 Patten Ave.
Ellenton, FL 34222
(941) 723-4536

Admission: *Free. Visits at the mansion are by tour only. Tour fees are $5 adults, $3 children 6 to 12, free for children younger than 6.*

Hours: *Thursday through Monday from 8 a.m. to sunset. Call for a tour schedule. No tours Tuesday or Wednesday. Tours leave at 9:30 a.m., 10:30 a.m., and on the hour from 1 p.m to 4 p.m.*

www.floridastateparks.org/ gambleplantation

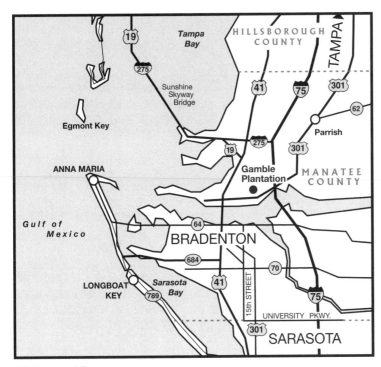

Directions

From Tampa, take Interstate 75 south to the U.S. 301 exit. Head west 1 mile and the entrance is on the right.

At every turn, a history lesson.

Linger Lodge
Restaurant & R.V. Resort

a little bit of everything

Relax on the deck of the Linger Lodge Restaurant, which overlooks the picturesque Braden River.

The trip

Nestled along the picturesque Braden River, this is the perfectly named place to linger awhile. For more than 60 years, visitors have come here to appreciate the area's pristine beauty, lush foliage and abundance of wildlife.

What to see

The setting is Old Florida at its best. There are more than 10 acres of peace and quiet at this R.V. resort. You can park your R.V. at one of the waterfront lots or park among the natural beauty of the palm and pine trees. The secluded Braden River flows along the south side, and it's a fishing paradise.

You don't need an R.V. to stop by. The unique restaurant has brought people here for years. Do they come for the grilled sandwiches and fried alligator? Well, yes. Hundreds of creatures — some more unusual than others — are mounted and on display in the restaurant.

Other highlights

Canoe daytrips along the river can be arranged at the nearby Canoe Outpost (813) 634-2228. Paddling along the Braden you might see wild boars, soft-shell turtles, native birds and plenty of alligators.

The facts

Linger Lodge Restaurant & R.V. Resort
7205 85th Street Court E. Bradenton, FL 34202
(941) 755-2757

Admission: *Call for lot rental rates.*

Office hours: *Monday through Friday 8:30 a.m. to 5 p.m., Saturday 9 a.m. to 1 p.m. In the summer, restaurant is open Wednesday through Thursday 11 a.m. to 8 p.m., Friday and Saturday 11 a.m. to 9 p.m. and Sunday 11 a.m. to 8 p.m. In winter, Monday through Saturday, 11 a.m. to 9 p.m., Sunday 11 a.m. to 8 p.m.*

www.lingerlodgeresort.com

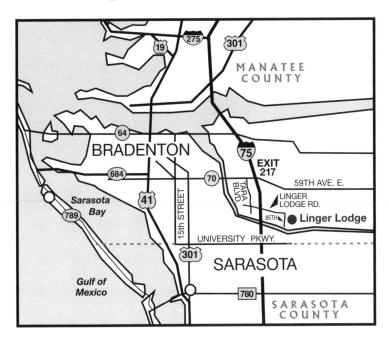

Beauty abounds here. It's a pleasant way to escape from it all.

Directions

From Tampa, take Interstate 75 to exit 217 (State Road 70 west). Make a left onto Tara Blvd., heading south. Turn left onto Linger Lodge Road. Turn right onto 85th Street Court.

South Florida Museum, Bishop Planetarium & Parker Manatee Aquarium

▼ 40

three for the price of one

The South Florida Museum is the home of manatees, memorabilia and magnificent stars.

The trip

This place is really three trips in one: the South Florida Museum, the Bishop Planetarium and the Parker Manatee Aquarium. There's so much to see and do that you'll have quite a day here.

What to see

The 118-seat planetarium is a wonder of planets and stars. The South Florida Museum lets you get close to the natural history of Florida from the Ice Age to the present. There are life-size casts of Ice Age mammals that roamed in Southwest Florida 12,000 years ago, and realistic dioramas and fossil exhibits that explain how Florida was formed.

Other highlights

You can journey back in time to Spain in the Spanish Plaza with its replica of a 16th century chapel. Not to be missed is the changing exhibits gallery where you never know what to expect, but you can count on it being fascinating and informative.

The facts

South Florida Museum
201 10th St. W.
Bradenton, FL 34205
(941) 746-4131

Admission: *$15.95 adults, $13.95 seniors 60 and older, $11.95 children 4 to 12, free for preschoolers with a paying adult.*

Hours: *Daily January through April and July, Monday through Saturday 10 a.m. to 5 p.m. Sundays noon to 5 p.m. All other months Tuesday through Saturday from 10 a.m. to 5 p.m. Sundays noon to 5 p.m. Closed Thanksgiving Day, Christmas Day and New Year's Day.*

www.southfloridamuseum.org

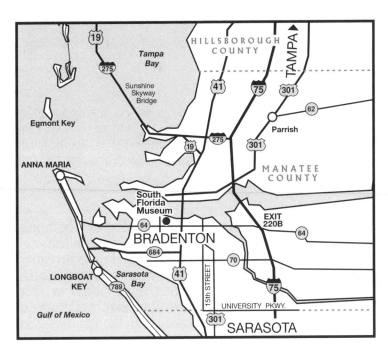

Directions

From Tampa, take Interstate 75 south to exit 220-B (State Road 64). Go west to 10th Street west and then right two blocks to the museum.

A wonder of planets, stars and natural history.

Ca' d'Zan, the Ringling Winter Residence

such elegance!

▼
41

John and Mable Ringling's winter residence was designed to evoke the splendor of Venetian Gothic palaces with columns in the courtyard and the sculpture of the Fountain of Oceanus.

John and Mable Ringling Museum of Art

The trip

The winter residence of John and Mable Ringling, set on scenic Sarasota Bay, is nothing short of magnificent. Stand on the terrace and soak in the spectacular view of the bay and barrier islands. Once inside, see how the rich and famous used to live. The house was featured in the film "Great Expectations" starring Gwyneth Paltrow.

What to see

Called Ca' d'Zan, or "House of John" in Venetian dialect, the house is 200 feet long, with 30 rooms and 15 baths. The home reflects the Ringlings' taste in architecture with its breathtaking style and attention to detail. It took two years to build their monument to Venetian palaces here on Florida's west coast. The house was finished in 1926 and cost about $1.5 million. Inside, explore the Ringlings' collection of furniture and paintings—a glimpse of the good life in the Roaring '20s.

Other highlights

Don't leave without a trip to the rest of the museum complex. More than 500 years of European art are on display in the fabulous museum. Love the circus? See the costumes, posters, props and circus wagons at the Circus Museum.

The facts

Ca' d'Zan, the Ringling Winter Residence
5401 Bay Shore Road
Sarasota, FL 34243
(941) 359-5700

Admission: $19 adults, $16 seniors,
$6 children 6 to 17, $6 Florida students and
teachers with valid ID, $6 active U.S. Military.

Hours: Daily 10 a.m. to 5:30 p.m.
Closed New Year's Day, Thanksgiving and
Christmas.

www.ringling.org

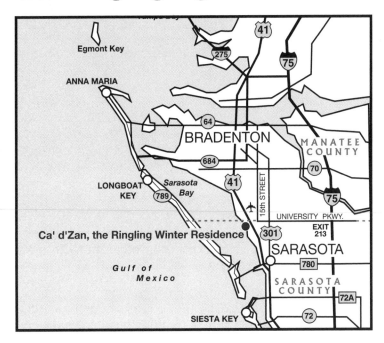

Directions

From Tampa, take Interstate 75 south to exit 213
(University Parkway) west to Sarasota until it ends at
the museum. The museum is at the intersection of
University Parkway and U.S. 41, just south of the
Sarasota-Bradenton International Airport.

The splendor
of the
Roaring '20s
is for all to
enjoy.

Historic Spanish Point

a walk through time

The rooms in the Guptill House, built in 1901 by Frank and Lizzie Webb Guptill, feature exhibits from the period.

The trip

This 30-acre site between Sarasota and Venice offers a fascinating history lesson. Exhibits take you from prehistoric times to the early 20th century.

What to see

You can start with ancient history. Go inside a midden or shell mound. These ancient "trash heaps," with tools, bones and other artifacts, are a virtual history book of native people from 2000 B.C. to 1000 A.D.

When you're ready for more modern times, head to the Guptill House. It's just one of a collection of buildings that let you explore pioneer life in Florida from 1867 to 1910. After you walk through the homestead house, visit the pioneer cemetery, chapel and citrus packing house.

Other highlights

From 1910 to 1918, Bertha Matilde Honore' Palmer left her own mark on Spanish Point — magnificent formal lawns and gardens designed around the pioneer dwellings and native remains. If you prefer a little wilderness in its natural state, walk along the nature trails.

The facts

Historic Spanish Point
337 N. Tamiami Trail
P.O. Box 846
Osprey, FL 34229
(941) 966-5214

Admission: *$9 adults, $8 seniors and Florida residents, $3 children 6 to 12, free for children 5 and younger.*

Hours: *Monday through Saturday 9 a.m. to 5 p.m., Sunday noon to 5 p.m. Closed on major holidays. Guided tours are offered daily. Call for tour times.*

www.historicspanishpoint.org

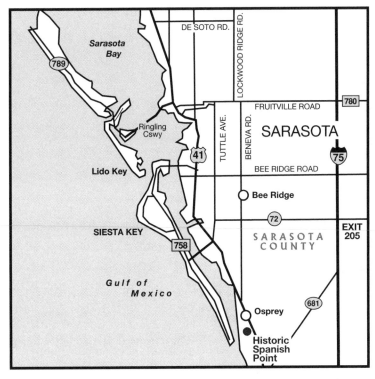

Directions

From Tampa, take Interstate 75 south to exit 205 (State Road 72). Head west 2.9 miles then turn left at Beneva Road. Head south for 2.4 miles then turn left on U.S. 41. Go south 2 miles; turn right at the Visitors Center.

5,000 years of history in one place.

Historic Spanish Point

Marie Selby Botanical Gardens

a treat for the eyes...and nose

Theophil Kuczynski

Marie Selby Botanical Gardens

The enchanting Dove or Holy Ghost orchid, above, and Butterfly orchid, left, are among the 6,000 orchids on display.

The trip

It's been called "a supernova in the constellation of botanical gardens." The beauty here is inescapable.

What to see

Selby Gardens is a living outdoor and under-glass museum of more than 20,000 plants, each of them more breathtaking than the last. At every turn, a photo opportunity awaits. Perhaps this place is best known for its living collection of more than 6,000 orchids. These treasures will steal your heart.

Other highlights

A stop by the Butterfly Garden is a must. And make sure you see the amazing banyan grove. It's almost as though arms and hands are reaching out to you from the roots and branches. Among the 20 distinct gardens are the spectacular bromeliad display, the palm grove and the koi pond.

The facts

Marie Selby Botanical Gardens
811 S. Palm Ave.
Sarasota, FL 34236
(941) 366-5731

Admission: $12 adults, $6 children 6 to 11, *free for children 5 and younger.*

Hours: Daily 10 a.m. to 5 p.m. *Closed Christmas Day.*

www.selby.org

Directions

From Tampa, take Interstate 75 to exit 210 (Fruitville Road). Proceed west about 7 miles to the end; turn left onto U.S. 301. Turn right on Mound Street (U.S. 41). Turn left onto South Palm Avenue. The entrance to the Gardens is at the end of the block on the right; parking is across from the entrance.

One of the most enchanting places you'll ever visit.

▼
44

Mote Marine
Laboratory & Aquarium

a "must see" in Sarasota

Mote Aquarium

This denizen of the deep is one of the more than 200 varieties of fish and invertebrates you can see at the aquarium.

The trip

Near St. Armands Circle in Sarasota, Mote Marine Laboratory & Aquarium is an extremely impressive collection of both unique and familiar sea life.

What to see

"Look, touch and explore" is the motto here. A 30-foot touch tank lets you do just that. Ever wondered what stingrays feel like? Here's your chance to find out. More than 20 viewing tanks display eels, turtles, starfish and sea plants. Mote Aquarium is also home to dolphins and manatees. Don't miss the 135,000-gallon outdoor shark habitat. It's a display with some teeth.

Other highlights

Visitors can get in touch with a working marine laboratory as they explore the secrets of the sea. Immersion Cinema and the interactive SHARKTRACKER exhibit allow visitors a glimpse of the high-tech tools used by researchers at the renowned Mote Marine Laboratory. Mote Aquarium also features trained docents situated throughout the aquarium who are always on hand to answer questions.

The facts

Mote Marine Laboratory & Aquarium
1600 Ken Thompson Parkway
Sarasota, FL 34236
(941) 388-4441

Admission: *$17 adults, $16 seniors, $12 children 4 to 12, free for children younger than 4. Annual membership available at $50.*

Hours: *Daily 10 a.m. to 5 p.m.*

www.mote.org

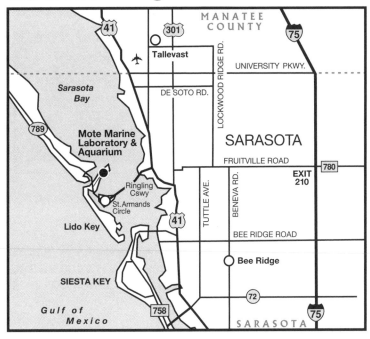

Directions

From Tampa, take Interstate 75 south to exit 210 (Fruitville Road). Head west to U.S. 41 south (Tamiami Trail). From U.S. 41, turn right at Gulfstream Avenue and proceed across the Ringling Causeway to St. Armands Circle. Exit the circle at North Boulevard of the Presidents. Proceed 1 mile to the traffic signal at Ken Thompson Parkway; turn right. Main parking for the aquarium will be on the right.

A fascinating underwater world awaits.

St. Armands Circle

a shopper's paradise

Sarasota Convention and Visitors Bureau

Stroll through the shops or relax in the restaurants that St. Armands Circle offers.

The trip

It's been called the Rodeo Drive of Florida. St. Armands Circle sits on St. Armands Key. The key was purchased by Charles St. Amand in 1893 for a whopping $21.71. But his name was misspelled in land deeds as St. Armands, and that name has stuck to the area ever since.

What to see

More than 150 shops and restaurants — offering everything from fine food to fabulous jewels to fashion to fun stuff for Fido — are nestled on St. Armands Circle. When you're done shopping, stroll along the shopping circle and admire the lush tropical landscaping.

Other highlights

Beautiful Lido Beach is a short walk away. After a day of shopping and eating, a sunset stroll or a moonlight horse drawn carriage ride is the perfect way to top off your visit. Visit the nearby Colony Beach Resort.

The facts

St. Armands Circle Association
300 Madison Drive, Suite 201
Sarasota, FL 34236
(941) 388-1554

Admission: *Free.*

Hours: *Store and restaurant hours vary. Most stores are open Monday through Saturday from 9:30 a.m. to 5:30 p.m., evenings and Sundays afternoons.*

www.starmandscircleassoc.com

Directions

From Tampa, take Interstate 75 south to exit 210 (Fruitville Road). Head west on State Road 780; turn left onto U.S. 41. Turn right on Gulfstream Avenue to St. Armands Key.

Sarasota Bay Explorers

an outdoor odyssey

Sarasota Bay Explorers/Mote Marine Lab

Guided tours are the perfect way to explore marine life.

The trip

A kayak trip with Sarasota Bay Explorers is a three-hour adventure of fun, exercise and education through Sarasota Bay to South Lido Park.

What to see

No experience is necessary for this tour. You'll get lessons from a pro. Just about anyone can pick up the art of kayaking pretty quickly and be ready to head for the water.

On the water, you'll hear from a naturalist about the area's wildlife. Paddling through the backwater is a perfect way to get an education about flora and fauna as well as benefit from a workout at the same time.

Other highlights

Sarasota Bay Explorers also offers sea life encounter tours of Sarasota Bay and Roberts Bay aboard a 40-foot pontoon boat. Or, you can design your own charter for up to six people aboard the 24-foot "Miss Explorer," which comes with a captain and a naturalist guide.

The facts

Sarasota Bay Explorers sail from Mote Marine Aquarium
1600 Ken Thompson Parkway
Sarasota, FL 34236
(941) 388-4200

Admission: *Kayak tours are $55 adults, $45 children 4 to 17; sea life encounter tours are $26 for adults, $22 for children 6 to 12; nature safari tours $40 adults, $35 for 6 to 12. Charters are $295 for three hours.*

Hours: *Kayak tours Monday through Friday from 9:30 a.m. to 12:30 p.m. or 2 p.m. to 5 p.m. Call for times for the daily sea life encounter tours and to make reservations for all other tours*

www.sarasotabayexplorers.com

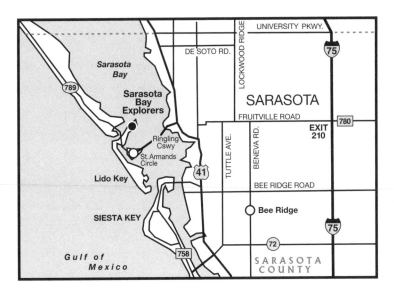

Directions

From Tampa, take Interstate 75 south to exit 210 (Fruitville Road). Head west to U.S. 41 and turn left. At Gulfstream Avenue turn right and proceed across the Ringling Causeway to St. Armands Circle. Exit the circle at North Boulevard of the Presidents. Proceed 1 mile; turn right at Ken Thompson Parkway. Main parking for the aquarium will be on the right.

An in-depth lesson on the water and along the banks of Sarasota Bay.

Sarasota Classic Car Museum

get your motor running

Sarasota Classic Car Museum

The Sarasota Classic Car Museum is the perfect stop for the chrome lover. The collection of cars is a tribute to engineering days gone by.

The trip

Within walking distance of the Ringling museum in Sarasota is another amazing collection of a different kind of art — classic cars.

What to see

This car museum displays the Beatles' cars — the psychedelic Bentley, John Lennon's 1965 Mercedes Benz 23SL convertible, and Paul McCartney's metallic green MINI Cooper. If you're a fanatic about fins, check out the '59 Cadillac El Dorado.

Other highlights

Visit the gift shop with its unique automobile-inspired souvenirs, rock'n'roll posters and t-shirts or have an outdoor picnic in the atrium. Check out the upscale shops at nearby St. Armand's Key.

The facts

Sarasota Classic Car Museum
5500 N. Tamiami Trail
Sarasota, FL 34243
(941) 355-6228

Admission: $8.50 adults, $7.65 seniors, $5.75
children 13 to 17, $4 children 6 to 12, free for children
5 and younger.

Hours: Daily 9 a.m. to 6 p.m.

www.sarasotacarmuseum.org

Directions

From Tampa, take Interstate 75 south to exit 213
(University Parkway). Head west to Sarasota. The museum
is at the intersection of University Parkway and U.S. 41.

Check
out the
"wheels" in
this museum.

Sarasota Jungle Gardens

it's a jungle out there!

Sarasota Jungle Gardens

Sarasota Jungle Gardens offers sanctuary and natural habitat for more than 200 animals from 70 different species, in addition to exotic bird and reptile shows.

The trip

Sarasota Jungle Gardens offers a truly tropical experience. There are plenty of birds to love — well, except for the gulls that that might eat your lunch. (Sorry, Charlie).

What to see

Snakes alive! This place has plenty of them, including the rare, and beautiful, Florida indigo snake. The daily reptile shows give you a chance to get personal with our scaly neighbors.

Other highlights

This is also a lemur-friendly neighborhood that is home to flamingos, monkeys and giant tortoises. Check out those feathered friends in the daily bird shows that feature cockatoos and macaws. And at holiday time, don't miss the "Holiday Lights, Jungle Nights" display. It runs from the night before Thanksgiving through December 31 annually.

The facts

Sarasota Jungle Gardens
3701 Bay Shore Road
Sarasota, FL 34234
(941) 355-1112

Admission: *$14 teens and adults, $13 seniors 62 and older, $10 children 3 to 12.*

Hours: *Daily 9 a.m. to 5 p.m. Closed Thanksgiving and Christmas Day.*

www.sarasotajunglegardens.com

This is a picture-taking paradise. Especially the birds!

Directions
From Tampa, take Interstate 75 south to exit 213 (University Parkway). Turn left on U.S. 41; turn right on Myrtle. Turn left onto Bay Shore Road.

Arcadia

old-fashioned friendliness

The Old Opera House sits on Polk Street in downtown Arcadia.

The trip

While some travel books call it "Cowboy Town," the lovely community of Arcadia is much more. One author named it "The Best Small Town in Florida," and a stroll through the charming historic district is proof.

What to see

Old town Arcadia boasts 20 antique and specialty shops, with plenty of charming collectibles and an abundance of friendly folks. And if you like architecture, the historic district includes some prime examples from the early 1900s. Your day trip should include lunch, of course, and there are plenty of restaurants to visit from ice cream shops to country cooking kitchens.

Other highlights

Stop by the Oak Ridge Cemetery. Twenty-three Royal Air Force cadets died while training in Florida during World War II. Their remains are here at a special British section of the cemetery where the Union Jack flies daily — young men forever.

The facts

Arcadia
DeSoto County
Chamber of Commerce
16 S. Volusia Ave.
Arcadia, FL 34266
(863) 494-4033

Admission: *Free.*

Hours: *Shop and restaurant hours vary.*

www.desotochamber.net

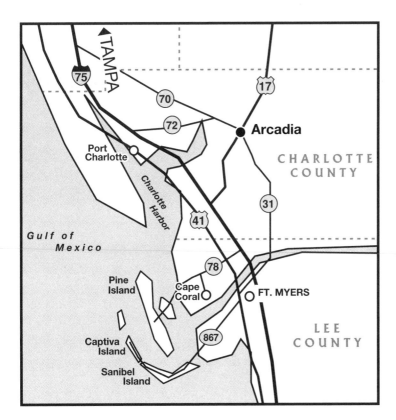

Directions

From Tampa, take Interstate 75 south to the State Road 70 exit. Follow S.R. 70 east about 40 miles to historic downtown Arcadia.

Arcadia has a homespun charm. You'll be pleasantly surprised and warmly greeted.

Canoe Outpost at Peace River

give peace a chance

A canoe or kayak trip down the Peace River is the perfect way to restore your peace of mind.

The trip

The adventure begins with a stop at the Canoe Outpost, a family-run business that was the first canoe outfitter in the state. From there it's a bus ride, canoes in tow, to the place where you start your "downstream" paddle on the Peace River.

What to see

The Peace River is one of the most beautiful paddle trails in the state. The river runs from the Green Swamp all the way to the Gulf of Mexico. It's more than 100 miles long, 63 miles are designated paddle trails.

You can take wilderness half- or full-day trips or stay out overnight along the river. Either way, make sure you take your time and enjoy the scenery. Don't worry about carrying your supplies. The folks at Canoe Outpost can get your gear to a designated campsite on some of the overnight trips.

Other highlights

Stop whenever you like along the river to swim, fish, hike or go fossil hunting. This is a great place to explore. And if you have time, visit nearby Arcadia, another **One Tank Trip**® destination.

The facts

Canoe Outpost at Peace River
2816 N.W. County Road 661
Arcadia, FL 34266
(800) 268-0083

Admission: *Leisure paddle $40 per canoe for 2 people, $10 for each additional person ages 13 and older. Free for children 12 and younger. A two-day/one-overnight leisure trip is $75 per canoe for two people.*

Hours: *Daily year-round. Call for weekday and weekend departure times.*

www.canoeoutpost.com/Peace/
peace1.html

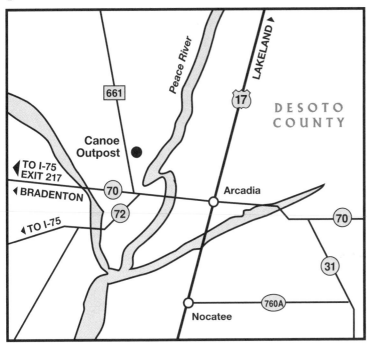

Directions

From Tampa, take Interstate 75 south to exit 217 (State Road 70) and head east for 39 miles. Turn north on County Road 661 at Peace River Campground. The Canoe Outpost is on the right behind the campground.

A
beautiful
river
that is
well-named.

Captiva Island

Florida's Tahiti

Lee Island Coast

Blind Pass separates the barrier islands, and stunning beaches, of Captiva and Sanibel.

The trip

You will love your visit to the barrier island of Captiva. The setting is picturesque and then some. Captiva and its sister island, Sanibel, offer incredible natural beauty.

What to see

Captiva Beach has been called "Florida's Most Romantic and Best Sunset Beach," and it's easy to see why. The sand and surf are glorious. And the shells! This is a shell collector's paradise, no matter the time of year. Sunrise is the best time to find a treasure.

Other highlights

For those who enjoy fishing, it's like dying and going to heaven. Bring your own pole and boat or arrange a charter. And stop by the Chapel by the Sea. This tiny chapel, once the one-room schoolhouse on the island, still is the site of worship services from November through April. Enjoy the many excellent restaurants.

The facts

Sanibel & Captiva Islands Chamber of Commerce
1159 Causeway Road
Sanibel Island, FL 33957
(239) 472-1080

Admission: *Free, although there is a $6 toll on the causeway. Beach-access parking is $2 an hour.*

Hours: *Public park beaches close at dusk. Restaurant, shop and attraction hours vary.*

www.sanibel-captiva.org

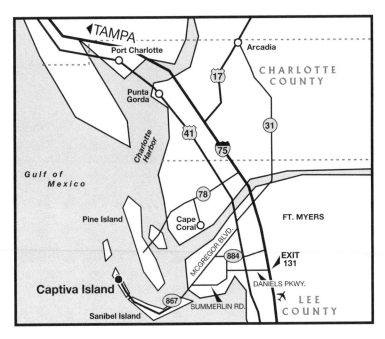

Directions

From Tampa, take Interstate 75 south to exit 131 (Daniels Parkway). Proceed west to Summerlin Road. Follow Summerlin Road across the Sanibel Causeway (a $6 toll) to Sanibel Island. At the four-way stop, turn right on Periwinkle Way. Turn right at Tarpon Bay and left on Sanibel-Captiva Road. Drive about 8 miles and cross Blind Pass Bridge and you're on Captiva Island.

From the beach, to a book, to a bite of lunch, this is indeed a wondrous place to get away from it all.

Edison & Ford Winter Estates

Lee County luxury

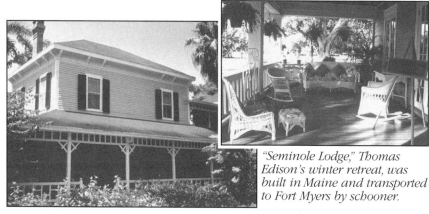

Edison-Ford Winter Estates

"Seminole Lodge," Thomas Edison's winter retreat, was built in Maine and transported to Fort Myers by schooner.

The trip

Henry Ford came to visit the Edisons in 1915. In 1916 he bought the house next door for his winter home. Together these two estates display the life and times of two remarkable families. Pay a visit to them and step back into a time when two modern geniuses lived and worked.

What to see

Edison loved this setting along the Caloosahatchee River. He would spend hours fishing off the pier — without any bait on the hook. He was here to think, not catch fish. He conducted his last major experiments in the laboratory here. Today, the lab looks about the same, with its test tubes and research. His "cat-nap" cot still sits in the lab, ready to be used.

Edison once said, "Of all my inventions, I like the phonograph best." Many are on display in the Edison Museum. You can also see his Model T Ford, a gift from friend Henry Ford.

Other highlights

The historic research and contemporary gardens consist of approximately 20 acres of lush tropical botanical gardens, 500 unique plants, flowers and trees, including four champion trees, the federal C.I.T.E.S. orchid program and propagation greenhouse and nursery. The remarkable gardens are included as part of the house and laboratory tours, but special botanical tours can be taken on Thursday and Saturday mornings.

The facts

Edison & Ford Winter Estates
2350 McGregor Blvd.
Fort Myers, FL 33901
(239) 334-7419

Admission: *$20 adults, $11 children 6 to 12, free for children younger than 6. Botanical tour $24 adults, $5 children 6 to 12.*

Hours: *Daily 9 a.m. to 5:30 p.m. Last guided tour leaves at 4 p.m. Botanical tours Thursday, Saturday 9 a.m.*

www.efwefla.org

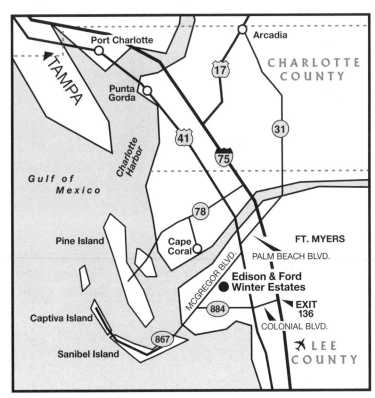

Directions

From Tampa, take Interstate 75 south to exit 136 (Colonial Boulevard, State Road 884). Turn right onto McGregor Blvd. Go approximately 2 miles, the Estates entrance is on the right.

This is the place where geniuses played.

WEATHER GUIDE

FOX 13 WEATHER
TM FOX

	Fort Myers		Jacksonville		Key West		Miami	
	High/Low	Rainfall	High/Low	Rainfall	High/Low	Rainfall	High/Low	Rainfall
January	74°/53°	1.8"	64°/42°	3.3"	75°/65°	2.0"	75°/59°	2.0"
February	76°/54°	2.2"	67°/44°	3.9"	75°/65°	1.8"	76°/60°	2.1"
March	80°/59°	3.1"	74°/50°	3.7"	79°/69°	1.7"	79°/64°	2.4"
April	85°/62°	1.1"	80°/56°	2.8"	82°/72°	1.8"	83°/68°	3.0"
May	89°/68°	3.9"	85°/63°	3.6"	85°/76°	3.5"	85°/72°	6.2"
June	91°/73°	9.5"	89°/70°	5.7"	88°/79°	5.1"	88°/75°	9.3"
July	91°/75°	8.3"	92°/73°	5.6"	89°/80°	3.6"	89°/77°	5.7"
August	91°/75°	9.7"	91°/72°	7.9"	89°/79°	5.0"	89°/77°	7.6"
September	90°/74°	7.8"	87°/70°	7.1"	88°/79°	5.9"	88°/76°	7.6"
October	86°/69°	2.9"	80°/60°	2.9"	84°/76°	4.4"	85°/72°	5.6"
November	81°/61°	1.6"	73°/50°	2.2"	80°/71°	2.8"	80°/67°	2.7"
December	76°/55°	1.6"	67°/44°	2.7"	76°/67°	2.0"	77°/62°	1.8"

	Orlando		Pensacola		Tampa Bay		Tallahassee	
	High/Low	Rainfall	High/Low	Rainfall	High/Low	Rainfall	High/Low	Rainfall
January	72°/51°	2.3"	60°/41°	4.7"	70°/49°	2.0"	63°/38°	4.8"
February	72°/50°	4.0"	63°/44°	5.4"	71°/51°	3.1"	66°/40°	5.5"
March	78°/56°	3.2"	69°/51°	5.7"	77°/56°	3.0"	73°/47°	6.2"
April	84°/61°	1.3"	76°/58°	3.4"	82°/61°	1.2"	80°/52°	3.7"
May	88°/67°	3.1"	83°/66°	4.2"	87°/67°	3.1"	86°/61°	4.8"
June	91°/72°	7.5"	89°/72°	6.4"	90°/73°	5.5"	91°/68°	6.9"
July	92°/74°	7.2"	90°/74°	7.4"	90°/74°	6.6"	91°/71°	8.8"
August	91°/74°	7.1"	89°/74°	7.3"	90°/74°	4.6"	91°/71°	7.5"
September	89°/73°	6.3"	86°/70°	5.4"	89°/73°	6.0"	88°/68°	5.6"
October	84°/67°	2.9"	79°/60°	4.1"	84°/65°	2.0"	81°/56°	2.9"
November	77°/57°	1.7"	70°/51°	3.5"	78°/57°	1.8"	73°/46°	3.9"
December	73°/52°	2.0"	63°/44°	4.3"	72°/52°	2.2"	66°/41°	5.0"

A Word About
The Weather

As you make your plans to travel around Florida using **One Tank Trips®: Fun Florida Adventures,** I thought you would like to know the average high and low temperatures and rainfall. For your convenience, I have prepared the accompanying chart to use as a reference.

For the most part, Florida weather is typically pleasant. In the summer, afternoon rains are almost a daily occurrence. But please be aware that there is always the possibility of dangerous lightning, tornadoes, floods and even hurricanes. Hurricane season begins in June and runs through the end of November. If a hurricane is approaching, I urge you to take watches and warnings seriously.

For the latest weather updates and information log onto **www.myfoxtampabay.com** where you will find SkyTower OMNI radar views along with our hurricane and severe weather guide. You can also use your mobile phone/PDA to see the latest SkyTower OMNI radar views. For additional hurricane information, log onto **www.myfoxhurricane.com**.

Here's wishing you lots of smiles and laughter and, above all, enjoy your travels!

Paul Dellegatto
WTVT FOX13 Chief Meteorologist

Sunshine State Sports

R. Rogers Tampa Bay Rays

Catch the excitement of a Tampa Bay Rays game at Tropicana Field in St. Petersburg.

D. Lowdermilk

Raymond James Stadium in Tampa is home to the Tampa Bay Buccaneers and the USF Bulls.

Tampa Bay Buccaneers

Watch the Lightning take the ice at the St. Pete Times Forum in Tampa.

A Word about Sports

In the Bay Area, you can cheer on our college and pro sports teams at some of the finest stadium facilities in the country. The University of South Florida has broken into the big time when it comes to NCAA football and Tampa is also the home of the ACC Championship game and the Outback Bowl.

"Fire the cannons!" The Tampa Bay Buccaneers and their famous pirate ship are a must see for the adventurous football fan. You can also cool your heels when the Tampa Bay Lightning heat up the ice or you could take a swing at Major League Baseball when the Tampa Bay Rays take the field in St. Petersburg. If you have a need for speed, you're just a tankful away from the biggest race in motor sports, the Daytona 500.

So, pick a sport, pick a spot to travel to, then pile the family in the car and enjoy a **One Tank Trip**® to some of the best athletic events in America.

Chip Carter
WTVT FOX13 Sports Director

SUNSHINE STATE SPORTS ATTRACTIONS

Major League Baseball – www.mlb.com
Florida Marlins, Dolphin Stadium, Miami
Tampa Bay Rays, Tropicana Field, St. Petersburg

Spring Training Baseball (Grapefruit League)
Atlanta Braves, Disney's Wide World of Sports, Kissimmee
Baltimore Orioles, Fort Lauderdale Stadium, Fort Lauderdale
Boston Red Sox, City of Palms Park, Fort Myers
Cincinnati Reds, Ed Smith Stadium, Sarasota
Cleveland Indians, Chain of Lakes Park, Winter Haven
Detroit Tigers, Joker Marchant Stadium, Lakeland
Florida Marlins, Roger Dean Stadium, Jupiter

Houston Astros, Osceola County Stadium, Kissimmee
Los Angeles Dodgers, Holman Stadium, Vero Beach
New York Mets, Tradition Field, Port St. Lucie
New York Yankees, Legends Field, Tampa
Philadelphia Phillies, Bright House Networks Field, Clearwater
Pittsburgh Pirates, McKechnie Field, Bradenton
Tampa Bay Rays, Charlotte Sports Park, Port Charlotte
Toronto Blue Jays, Knology Park, Dunedin

National Basketball Association – www.nba.com
Orlando Magic, Orlando Arena, Orlando
Miami Heat, American Airlines Arena, Miami

National Football League – www.nfl.com
Tampa Bay Buccaneers, Raymond James Stadium, Tampa
Jacksonville Jaguars, Alltel Stadium, Jacksonville
Miami Dolphins, Dolphin Stadium, Miami

Arena Football League – www.arenafootball.com
Tampa Bay Storm, St. Pete Times Forum, Tampa
Orlando Predators, Orlando Arena, Orlando

National Hockey League – www.nhl.com
Tampa Bay Lightning, St. Pete Times Forum, Tampa
Florida Panthers, National Car Rental Center, Miami

NASCAR and International Racing – www.nascar.com
Daytona International Speedway, Daytona Beach
Homestead-Miami Speedway, Homestead
USA International Speedway, Lakeland
Sebring International Raceway, Sebring

College Athletics
Bethune-Cookman University, Daytona Beach
Florida A&M University, Tallahassee
Florida State University, Tallahassee
University of Florida, Gainesville
University of Central Florida, Orlando
University of Miami, Coral Gables
University of South Florida, Tampa

I N D E X